MANY HEA

© G C Davies 1995

First published 1995 by
Nash Pollock Publishing
32 Warwick Street
Oxford OX4 1SX

10 9 8 7 6

Orders to:
York Publishing Services
64 Hallfield Road
Layerthorpe
York YO3 7XQ

A catalogue record of this book is available from the British Library

ISBN 1 898255 05 9

Typeset in 11 on 13pt Galliard by Black Dog Design, Buckingham
Cover illustration by Clare Mattey
Printed in Great Britain by T.J. International Ltd, Padstow

MANY HEARTS

An Assembly Book for 4–8 year olds

Geoff Davies

NASH POLLOCK PUBLISHING

Acknowledgements

I am grateful to my wife Mollie, for reading the stories and for her patience, to Terry Dillon, Headteacher, St Mary's C E School, Kintbury, and to my son-in-law Richard Hollingum, of the South Oxfordshire College of Education, for their invaluable help.

Copyright acknowledgements

Franklin Watts Ltd for 'How Sad' by William Cole; Mrs Ian Seraillier for 'First Foot'; Oxford University Press for paraphrased extract from *Lark Rise to Candleford* by Flora Thompson; Abingdon Press for 'Thanksgiving' by Ivy O Eastwick; David Higham Associates for extract from *Under Milk Wood* by Dylan Thomas.

Contents

ALL AROUND US

THIS AND THAT

LEARNING AND GROWING

SPECIAL DAYS – TRADITIONAL CELEBRATIONS

Assembly

SPECIAL DAYS ORIGINATING IN CULTURES NOT NATIVE TO THE UNITED KINGDOM

Assembly

APPENDICES

About this book

This book suggests a range of themes that can be used for assemblies with children in Reception, Y1 and Y2 (and, adapted, for Y3 in First Schools), whatever the population mix of the school may be.

Part 1 offers 68 topics, most with a thinly disguised moral. Part 2 comprises 18 festivals, eleven subjects traditional to the United Kingdom and seven that find their origins beyond these shores. The stories are a mixture of anthropomorphic adventures, the misdemeanours of Little People, the Inexplicable Intervention of a Mary Poppins type of Old Lady, and reality or neo-reality (such as the Belloc type characters to be encountered in verse). Most children enjoy, and are unaffected by, innocent fantasy at this level. All stories, poems and narratives take about three minutes to read or tell, unless, of course, you wish to embellish them in any way.

Unlikely forenames have been chosen so as to reduce the possibility of individual children being compared to any characters who may exhibit undesirable traits.

Stories and Narratives are preceded with suggestions to start the assembly. *Starters* are offered to bridge the gap where the conducting teacher wishes to involve the children verbally and to give an element of dialogue if this is wanted. The stories and narratives can, of course, be told with no introduction or follow-up – it depends how teachers wish to use them.

Teachers know what is the purpose behind an assembly – in Infant schools they are usually custom-built to match current circumstances – immediacy being the keynote of the world of the under-eight child – but the suggestions are there for anyone who wishes to pick them up. The assemblies are not intended to be complete recipes, but rather offering a range of ingredients from which teachers can select material that suits their particular requirements.

Each assembly has a section suggesting suitable songs and monotheistic prayers. The only reference to Jesus Christ is in the two Christmas assemblies. The assemblies for other Christian feasts look at traditional activities that have no direct religous implication.

Each non-Christian festival is marked with a story that has no origin in the mother culture of that faith. Hindu, Jewish, Muslim and Buddhist children already enjoy a wealth of stories related to their own faiths, which, no doubt, they will encounter during their own religious education, in and out of school. These assemblies do not attempt to teach children about the non-Christian faiths – the statutory requirements for religious education place such teaching firmly in the classroom and not in the assembly situation.

Poetry, providing extra reading for 'Special Occasions', is gathered in Appendix 1 on page 198.

Mood music ('coming-in' and 'going-out') is suggested in Appendix 2 on page 208. It would be unrealistic to expect teachers to use recorded material unless it is readily available in school or (as so often) in their own personal music resources.

Suggestions for *Songs* are drawn from the song books currently best-known and used most frequently in Infant or First schools, and most songs are repeated at intervals. They are of course no more than suggestions, and teachers may well prefer to make their own selections, either from the same song books or from different books. The titles and sources are collected in Appendix 3 on page 214, for those teachers who do not wish to plough through assemblies to find the song they want.

A *Thought to share* is included in each assembly for those teachers who prefer to avoid 'prayers' for any reason. The *Prayers* ('Are you listening, God?') are addressed to a deity unrelated to any particular faith or denomination. Some prayers are repeated at intervals. Other and different prayers are, for convenience, to be found in Appendix 4 on page 220. Two versions of The Lord's Prayer are to be found at the end of the Appendix. The first version has been rewritten to be more meaningful for Infant children and the second is taken directly from the *New English Bible*, second edition, 1970.

Many Hearts seeks to be non-contentious – religious education and the traditional collective act of worship is a curricular area that can cause problems to teachers and headteachers alike. Some educationists have suggested that school assemblies should be abandoned altogther. This would be a drastic step – we have no way of assessing whether a school ethos will be affected if the child and adult population no longer gathers together with a common purpose – whether the meeting is for whatever worship is deemed appropriate or whether it is some other collective act of thought. Gatherings to announce the date of Sports Day or the next PTA meeting are not likely to have the same atmosphere as an assembly that has a serious aim. It is hoped that this book will offer ideas for serious aims approached through material that is not too ponderous.

Daily life – school and home

1 This is our school

Theme
Welcome to new arrivals

Aim
Reassuring new children and showing them that starting school is not as bad as they might have thought. Many new children will have been to school on pre-school visits for 'familiarisation' but still need some reassurance. Ex-nursery school/class/unit children may also need some help in adjusting to a different environment, ethos, teachers and ancillary staff.

This material is intended for a whole Infant School or Department gathering in which Reception, Year 1 and Year 2 are participating, and assumes it is the first time that all Reception children are present. But no two schools are the same...

Starters
If you haven't already thought of it, introduce the teachers and any ancillary staff you can muster, to new arrivals.

Introduce any new staff to everybody (if that is your school policy).

Summing up
School can be a daunting place but everyone is there to help.

Story

Goldfish Number Five and a New Home

'Come along, Number Five,' said Boss Goldfish, looking out of the big tank in the pet shop, 'Mr Chum is coming with his net.'

Number Five was sad at the thought of leaving the big tank in the shop – she had never known any other home. The little red fish knew, though, that sooner or later she would have to live somewhere else.

Mr Chum scooped out Number Five very carefully and tipped her into a plastic bag, half-full of clear water. He gave the bag to a little boy whose name was Ryan. Ryan carried his new pet to the car, the bag going *Floppety flip, wibble wobble.* In the car, the bag went *Flippety flop, wobble wibble,* on William's lap, which he found rather funny.

Number Five was not worried by this. She was more worried about the fish she would meet in her new tank. 'What will it be like?' she wondered. 'Will the fish already there be friendly, or will they chase me round the tank?

'And what if there is a big bully fish who will be rough and rub off my scales and eat all the food before I can get any and I will starve to death? Oh, dear, I'm not going to like this. I want to go home.'

But before Number Five could think of any more dreadful things that *might* happen, she was being tipped into a beautiful tank with plants and shells in it.

The four goldfish who lived in it already were about the same size as Number Five. They told her that Ryan hardly ever forgot to put just the right amount of food in the tank – not too much, not too little, but just right. If he forgot, a grown-up would always remember.

They gave her a name, too – Ruby, because she was such a pretty shade of red. What a much prettier name than boring old Number Five.

Ruby could not think why she had been so nervous about starting off in her new home. She had imagined all sorts of dreadful things and none of them had happened at all. Come to think of it, the grown-ups did not sound too bad, either. Rather like starting in a new school, I suppose. Only you aren't goldfish!

Songs

For the beauty of the earth	*New Child Songs* 89
Morning has broken	*Someone's Singing, Lord* 3
Thank you for my friends	*Tinderbox* 31

A thought to share

Let us remember that a school is a place built for children.

Are you listening, God?

Please, God, show us how to help those children who are starting school today.

Father, help us to make our new teachers and helpers feel welcome in our school.

Thank you, Lord, for the holidays that are now over.

2 Many hands make a school

Theme

Many people are needed to make a school function

Aim

To help the children, especially the new pupils, understand that a school can only function properly because many people do many different jobs.

Starters

Identify yourself (name and status of the person conducting assembly).
  Identify the names of the teachers.
  Identify the names of key ancillary staff (NTA's, kitchen, domestic etc).
  The consequences if any of these people did not do their jobs properly, for whatever reason.

Summing up

Everyone is important, otherwise the school would not be the place it is (use your imagination...). You may prefer to deal with the wider aspects of the subject at classroom level, particularly in a large school. Here, you can broaden the theme to other people who are involved in running a school but are not members of staff, for example, medical and welfare staff. The older children may know about governors and parental involvement.

Story

Mr Stuffy buys a School

Mr Stuffy had always wanted to own a school. So he bought one. It was an old, small school and parents paid for their children to go there. Do you know of any schools like that? (Teacher: Use your discretion here.)

When Mr Stuffy moved in he found that there were only two teachers and they were both old and grumpy. He told them to go and teach in another school. So they did.

Although Mr. Stuffy was very rich, he was very mean. He said he would teach all the children himself. He also said he would get up early in the morning and stoke the boiler.

He also said he would do the cleaning and empty the litter bins every day. He told the caretaker to go and look after another school. So the caretaker did. (Teacher: You may have to substitute for 'caretaker'.)

Mr Stuffy said that his wife would cook the school dinners (lunches) and he would do the washing-up. He told the school cook to go and cook in a take-away shop or somewhere. So she did.

Mr Stuffy said Mrs Stuffy would deal with all the money, pay all the bills and type all the letters. He told the school secretary to go and get a job in an office somewhere. So she did.

After about a month of cooking, dealing with money, paying all the bills and typing all the letters, Mrs Stuffy got fed up. So she left the school and went back to her old house.

Of course, Mr Stuffy could not look after everything on his own. By this time, the parents did not like their children being taught in a class of a hundred children in a dirty, cold school.

Not only this, but all they got for school dinners were apples and crisps. As you might expect, the parents soon took their children away and sent them to other schools.

Which meant that Mr Stuffy had no teachers, no caretaker, no cook, no school secretary and, most important of all, no wife.

So he sold the school to the owner of a riding-stable.

Mr Stuffy had learned that nobody can run a school without people who know what they are doing. What is more, a school is of no use at all if there are no children in it!

Songs

If you're happy	*Apusskidu* 1
Hands to work and feet to run	*Someone's Singing, Lord* 21
O Lord, shout for joy!	*Someone's Singing, Lord* 4

A thought to share

Let us think about all the people who look after us in our school.

Are you listening, God?

Thank you, Father, for our school and all who work and play here.

Dear God, please make our school a safe and happy place.

Father God, help us make our school a place where we can all enjoy learning and playing.

3 Many hearts make a school

Theme

A school creed

Aim

Beginning the process of learning a modified version of a well-known School Creed that should be acceptable to all faiths.

You will see a 'School Creed' in other assembly books but the one presented here is adapted from what is probably the best-known version. The original is based on a verse first used in a one-room school in Canada, but this version has been devised to use more modern words, e.g. 'live' for 'dwell', and 'abide' and 'happiness' for 'contentment', the older words probably being rather mystifying for many of the younger children.

Learning the School Creed is best done by traditional rote. A good way of beginning memorisation may be to ask the children to repeat each line aloud after you. Repeat the exercise frequently and arrange for it to be followed up in the classroom – at frequent intervals.

Even the youngest children appear to have no problems in remembering the words which remain with many children for a long time. Many schools repeat a version of the Creed at frequent intervals instead of prayers.

If you have not used a School Creed before, it can be most worthwhile as an act of togetherness in which all can participate. You might prefer to write your own instead of using this one.

Narrative

*Use your discretion as to whether you include these leading questions or not. It depends on how vociferous your children are...

When a builder builds a house, he can't do it all by himself unless it is a very small house, he has a lot of time and he (or she) is a very clever person. The house will be built more quickly, and probably be built better, if the builder has other people to work with him.

It is important that they all know exactly what they are doing. The people who help to build houses work at what are called *trades*. For example, to build a house with bricks, you must have bricklayers, and we say that bricklaying is a trade.

*Who can tell me more about the people who build houses?

We have to build a school in the same way. I don't mean the building itself – that was done by people like those who build houses. I mean, those people who work so hard to make a school a happy and friendly place where you can learn.

*Who can tell me about the people who might do this?

All the people who work hard in school are very important, but the most important builders of a school are... you!

*Why?

Now we shall say a verse that I want you all to learn. It is called 'The School Creed' and it is a verse in which we say what kind of place we would like our school to be. (There is no need to explain the meaning of the word 'Creed'.)

We shall say it a line at a time. Say each line after me.

The School Creed

This is our school,
Let peace live here.
Let the rooms be full of happiness.
Let love be all around,
Love of one another,
Love of all people,
And love of life and living.
Let us remember
That as many hands build a house,
So many hearts make a school.

Songs

A house is a house for me	*Tinderbox* 13
I've just moved into a new house	*Tinderbox* 51
The building song	*Alleluya* 59

Thoughts and Prayers are not included in this assembly.

4 Do you know where you live?

Theme

Addresses

Aim

Emphasising the importance of children actually knowing their home address as well as being able to find their way home.

You are probably aware that some children do not know what their home address is and, even if they do, it does not always mean that they could find their way home if they were in difficulty.

Starters

Do the children know where they live?

Can they describe their dwellings and where they are?

Do they know how to get there?

(The topic is worth following up in the classroom – it is an important subject.)

Story

Herbert goes to the fair

'Where are you going, Herbert?' said Mrs. Hedgehog to her youngest son. But the little hedgehog had gone, scuttling up the road as fast as his little pink feet would carry him.

There was a fair in nearby Prickletown and Herbert had never been to a fair. His friend Hilda had told him about fairs – the roundabouts, the rides and, best of all, the roller-coaster.

Herbert hurried along. He didn't really know the way to the fair but, after walking for a while, he heard music. The little hedgehog stopped for a moment, listening. Then he headed towards the magical sound, scurrying faster and faster in the hot sunshine, the music getting louder all the time.

When he arrived at the fair Herbert could hardly believe his eyes. He had never seen anything so wonderful. He watched dodgem cars crashing into one another, their rabbit-drivers giggling stupidly like all rabbits do when they are excited.

Herbert stood with his mouth open as the swing-boats went up and down and the roundabouts of painted horses galloped around and around, never going anywhere. And the music played so loudly. It was all so exciting.

He held up his little pink paws in wonder and gasped, 'Oh, prickles and paws. Oh, my. Oh, my. How absolutely, stupendously prickleful!' And then he saw the roller coaster with its little cars swooping and rushing, their passengers screaming with the thrill of it. It was so wonderful, he could not speak at all.

Herbert wandered about for hours, just watching. Then, suddenly, he felt very tired and hungry. He asked Hiram Hare for some of the fluffy pink candy-floss that he was selling; but the hare laughed nastily when Herbert said he had no money.

So the little hedgehog decided to make his way home. But, oh dear – Herbert had no idea how to find his way home to 3 Flower Lane, Leafyton. There was no music to guide him, he had no idea which road to take and he had no money to catch a bus, if there was one that went to Leafyton. Whatever was he to do?

Herbert began to cry but nobody took any notice of the sobbing hedgehog. Then PC Badger saw him and asked him for his address. Herbert had no idea, except that he lived in Leafyton. He had been told his address many times by his Mum and Dad but he had never bothered to listen to them.

The policeman made a lot of phone calls, and it was late that night before Herbert was tucked up in his own little bed.

Do you know *your* address? Herbert does – now!

Songs

Can't help but wonder	*Alleluya* 34
Place to be	*Tinderbox* 34
Welcome home	*Tinderbox* 60

A thought to share

There is no place like home and we should be glad we have one.

Are you listening, God?

Father God, help us to find our way if ever we get lost.

Thank you, God, who made us,
For all your loving care,
For home and school and friends
And all the world so fair.

5 Left or right?

Theme

Left and right

Aim

To reinforce classroom activity in which children are taught to know left from right.

Starters

Which is left and and which is right? (...hands, legs etc, areas of the room and other points of orientation and direction of rotation)

How many children are left-handed? (if they know – not all do)

Can any children use *either* hand equally well? (The word 'ambidextrous' has been known to surface...)

Why is it important to know left from right?

Which way do we read European books; books from other languages (Chinese, Arabic)?

(Or deal with it at greater length in the classroom.)

Story

The Soldiers of King Munch's Army

Sergeant Snap puffed out his chest, straightened his big, black, furry hat (which is called a bearskin) and shouted at the twelve soldiers of King Munch's Army. Yes, you're quite right. It *is* a small Army.

'Now, today I am going to teach you to salute properly,' said the Sergeant (he has three stripes on each arm). He saluted smartly. As his arm went up and down, he shouted,'Up two three, down two three.' Have you seen soldiers doing this?

'Right,' said the Sergeant, 'All Together – Salute! Up, two three... He stopped and looked at the soldiers There was something wrong with some salutes. Privates Pop, Gulp and Chew were saluting with... their *left* hands. The Sergeant looked as if he was going to burst.

'What sort of salutes are those?' he yelled. 'Saluting with your left hands, indeed!'

Sergeant Snap made them march about for *hours*, shouting, 'Left turn, Right turn,' until the soldiers felt dizzy.

Private Pop fell in the castle moat. He had turned left instead of right. Private Swallow marched into the Royal Pigsty because he had turned right instead of left. Private Gobble started to cry because he was so muddled. Sergeant Snap got so fed up that he sent all the soldiers to bed without any cocoa and biscuits.

Next morning, Captain Crackle made the soldiers line up. He twiddled his moustache and said, 'Now, soldiers, it's awfully easy to remember which is your left hand and which is your right hand. Your *right* hand is the one you *write* letters with. The other hand is your left hand. Simple, isn't it?'

Corporal Smart coughed and said, 'Sir. What if you write with your left hand?'

Captain Crackle said, 'Oh. Ah. Hum. Good question, Corporal. I'll just go and ask General Crunch,' and he marched off to his office, whistling a marching tune.

When he had gone, Corporal Smart said, 'Who doesn't know their left hands from their right?' Privates Pop, Chew, Gulp, Swallow and Gobble put up their hands. Then with a felt pen, he wrote *Right* on the back of each soldier's right hand and *Left* on the back of each one's left hand. He told them not to wash the backs of their hands for two days, until they had learnt which hand was left and which hand was right. And, do you know, it worked! All the soldiers learnt which was which and never had any trouble after that.

I wonder, do you know *your* left from *your* right?

Songs

Kaigal – hands	*Tinderbox* 4
I've got a body	*Tinderbox* 5
Turn, turn, turn	*Alleluya* 32

A thought to share

Let us do our best to understand all the lessons we are taught.

Are you listening, God?

Father God, show us how to learn and ask for help if we need it.

Please, God, help us to do the things we should,
To be to others kind and good.

Father, help us to learn as much as we can.

6 Early to bed

Theme

Going to bed at a sensible time

Aim

To impress upon children the value of a good night's sleep if they are to perform well in daily life.

Starters

Too many children stay up too late – *fact*.

Which children went to bed at seven/eight o'clock last night (answers will probably depend on the time of year)?

Is ten o'clock too late? (etc.) (Many children will be proud of going to bed at a late hour – best followed up in the classroom.)

Some children look tired (some of them must do).

Summing up

What is wrong with being tired? Work or play cannot be done properly if a person is tired.

Worse than that, a tired person is not alert.

Poem

The Sad Story of Fred who Did Not Like Going to Bed

There was a boy whose name was Fred
Who did not like to go to bed.
However loud his mother screamed,
He would not go to bed to dream.
When Father said 'It's time to go,'
Young Freddy stamped and said, 'No, no!'
His parents moaned – it was no good,
The boy stood like a lump of wood.
He said, 'I want to watch TV again
I'll be asleep by half-past ten.'
His granny then began to speak,
'You've said the same thing for a week!'
Fred answered, 'I don't want to snore,
I think that sleeping is a bore.
If I watch late there is no harm,
And I will set my clock alarm.

I know I won't be late for school,
I'm seven years old and I'm no fool.'
He watched the screen with glassy stare
And fell asleep in Grandma's chair.
At breakfast time, he watched still more,
His mother said, 'It's time to go'
Our Fred, full up with ham and eggs,
Set off for school on shaky legs.
But on the way he met his doom
He didn't hear the bus come, *Brroom!*
The boy was flattened like a flea.
His father said, 'Well, don't blame me.'
His mother, who was quite put out,
Said, 'I'm sure that there can be no doubt.
If Fred had got a good night's sleep
He wouldn't be there in that heap.
If he'd gone to bed when he was told
He might have lived 'til he was old.
Without his sleep, he was not smart,
We should have known it from the start.'
So, children, try to get your rest
And you'll grow up – and be the best.

Songs

All night, all day	*Alleluya* 75
Hey ho! Time to go to bed	*Flying a Round* 14
Song of the Clock	*Tinderbox* 7

A thought to share

Think quietly about how important it is to be able to have a good
night's sleep.

Are you listening, God?

Father God, thank you for the sleep that we need to grow into strong and healthy people.

Dear God, help us to understand that grown-ups often know better than children.

Father, help us to do what we are asked to do without complaining too much.

7 Too much TV is bad for your health

Theme

The bad effect of watching too much TV

Aim

Encouraging children to watch less television.

Starters

How much time do children spend in watching TV?

What kind of programmes do they watch?

What is good about TV? What is bad about TV?

What is a 'couch potato'? (Indeed, what's a couch?)

Should TV be watched because it's there?

Summing up

Is it really bad for children to watch an inordinate amount of TV particularly when the viewing is indiscriminate and often uncensored?

Poem

The sad tale of Cyril Popkin

Cyril Popkin watched all programmes,
News, commercials and much more,
Watching from a comfy settee,
And, if he fell off, from the floor.
His mother said, 'Go out to play!
Or else your eyes will soon be square.'
But Cyril didn't hear a word
Or else the boy just did not care.
Then, one day, poor Cyril found
He could not get up from his seat.
He could not from the settee move,
He could not move his legs or feet.
Now, I must tell you, children dear,
Cyril Popkin is still there.
His worried parents dare not move him,
He can only sit and stare.
They feed him crisps, with Coke to drink,
He sips and chews and sips and stares,
The doctor says, 'You must not move him,
And he can never go upstairs.'
You should learn from this sad story,
That like poor Cyril you could be;
So please find something else to do.
And not just goggle at TV.

Poem

How Sad

There's a pitiful story – ah, me!
Of a young English girl named Nellie,
Who stared dumbly all day at TV
(Which in England is known as the tele)
She died. . . and the reason, you see,
Was her brains had all turned into jelly.

William Cole

Songs

For all the strength we have	*New Child Songs* 30
	& Someone's Singing, Lord 16
I've got a body	*Tinderbox* 5
The world is big, the world is small	*Tinderbox* 33

A thought to share

Let us imagine what we would do if TV had never been invented.

Are you listening, God?

Father God, thank you for all the wonderful inventions that make our lives such fun.

Dear God, help us to be sensible about using TV and video games.

Father of us all, please teach us how to make the best use of our time.

8 Matches are not toys

Theme

Danger – Fire!

Aim

To reinforce classroom and other activity that aims at educating children about the hazards of playing with matches or other means of combustion.

Starters

What are the risks of playing with matches/cigarette lighters etc.?

Are there other things that can catch fire when played with?

(Many schools invite Fire Service officers to talk about their work and other related topics. Approach the whole subject with caution – some children can be very distressed by too big an emphasis on the effects of fire.)

Story

Kendal Kangaroo and a Strange Box

Kendal is a little grey joey, which is what all young kangaroos in Australia are called. I am sorry to tell you that he often does things without thinking first.

He was out in the bush near Woomaloomoo one day when he discovered, under a eucalyptus tree, a bright yellow box. Kendal had never seen anything like it before.

He knew that humans had some strange things, like bush-hats and boomerangs and didgeree-doos and tucker-bags, and he never really understood why they wanted funny things like that, anyway.

But this box was something that puzzled the little kangaroo. On it was a picture of a blue ship, sailing in a yellow sea. Kendal had no idea what a ship was because he lived a very long way from the sea.

The joey picked up the box in both paws. It was not very heavy, not even for small kangaroos. He shook it. It rattled in a most exciting way.

What could it be? Then Kendal noticed that one side of the box was rough, even rougher than a grandad koala bear's fur.

He licked the box – it tasted like wood and was not at all pleasant. The rough side tasted worse than the other side.

Then Kendal sniffed the box and, while he was sniffing, it opened. His nose had pushed out a little tray. And there, in the tray, were a lot of little white sticks, each one with a red tip. Kendal shook the box and some sticks fell out.

One stuck to his paw, so he tasted it. Yik! Yuk! It tasted much worse than the box had. The little kangaroo rubbed a stick on the box. Nothing happened.

Then he rubbed it on the rough side of the box. And *you* can guess what happened, can't you? It burst into flame. Kendal squealed with fright and threw the stick away. It landed on some dry grass which caught fire, straight away.

It set light to an old dried-up tree stump. Soon, there were flames all around, growing higher and higher. Kendal did the only thing he could. He hopped away, like any sensible kangaroo.

In no time at all these flames became a dreadful bush fire. Many animals had to run for their lives or be rescued by bush-rangers. It took five days for firemen to put out the blaze.

Of course, Kendal didn't know what he had done. How could he? He is only a kangaroo joey. But *you* know what he had done. Without knowing it, he had played with matches. And look what happened.

And we know that matches are not toys – for kangaroos or for anyone else.

Songs

Can anyone tell me that?	*Tinderbox* 6
Mysteries	*Tinderbox* 40
Think, think on these things	*Someone's Singing, Lord* 38

A thought to share

Think about how we can keep away from danger and how we can help other children to do the same.

Are you listening, God?

Father God, please help us to understand what is right and what is wrong.

Please, God, show us how to behave sensibly.

Lord, give us the good sense to know what are foolish and dangerous games.

9 They may look like sweets

Theme

Coloured tablets can be dangerous.

Aim

To reinforce earlier teaching that eating unknown tablets can be dangerous.

Although ingesting dangerous substances is usually associated with pre-school children there are too frequent cases of children of school age being tempted by attractive pills or liquids.

Starters

Name a medicine.

Name a medicine that is found in tablet/pill form.

Can pills and tablets look like something else? (looking for: Smarties or M & M's type sweets)

What should be done if tempting-looking tablets are available?

What might happen if pills or unknown liquids are ingested?

Story

Trixie and the Sweets

Trixie was bored. Dad was chopping carrots for dinner and he did not want any help, especially from Trixie.

'When is Mummy going to be allowed to get up?' she said to her father. Her mother had been in bed for a week after hurting her back at an aerobics class.

'Oh soon, poppet,' said Dad, 'just as soon as the doctor says it is all right. Why don't you go and keep her company while I do this? Then perhaps we can go shopping.'

It was too cold to go out to play. Trixie did not like what was on TV and she'd seen all her videos ten times. She had broken her new Sindy doll and had looked at her books twice. She had only looked at the pictures, because she could not read very well yet.

So, as she could not think of anything else to do, she decided she would go and see her mother. Perhaps her Mum might even tell her a story about when she was a little girl – these were Trixie's favourite stories. Up the stairs she went and peeped round the bedroom door.

'Mummy,' she said, quietly. Her mother did not answer. Trixie went into the bedroom and tip-toed up to the bed. 'Mummy,' she said again, a little more loudly. She was very annoyed when her mother began to snore.

'Oh, bother,' said Trixie. 'Fancy her going to sleep. Just as I came in to see her. It's not fair.'

Then she saw something very interesting on the bedside cabinet. It was a small bottle full of what looked like red sweets. The bottle had a label on it, but Trixie's reading was not good enough to read what it said. Still, the sweets looked jolly good. 'Oo, Yum, Smarties. All red ones.' The top of the bottle came off easily and she tipped all the sweets on to the carpet. There seemed to be plenty there. Surely Mummy wouldn't miss a few. Trixie was just about to pop a handful into her mouth when a scream came from the bed.

'Don't you dare put them in your mouth!' Her mother had woken up and seen what Trixie was about to do. The four-year old threw the sweets down and began to cry.

'Oh, Trixie, I didn't mean to frighten you,' said her mother, holding out her arms to cuddle her. 'But those aren't sweets, darling. They are Mummy's pain killers for her bad back. You must never, ever eat pills that look like sweets, because they might make you very ill.'

Of course, Trixie's mother was quite right. But you are too old and too sensible to do anything like that. Aren't you?

Songs

Can anyone tell me that?	*Tinderbox* 6
How do you feel today?	*BBC Play School Song Book* 1
Paint box	*Harlequin* 32

A thought to share

Think quietly about all those who care for us and keep us safe and free from harm.

Are you listening, God?

Thank you, Father, for all those people who look after us if we have an accident.

Please, God, give us the sense to know what is good and what is bad in everything we do.

Father, teach us to be sensible children.

10 Staying away

Theme

Absenteeism

Aim:

Suggesting that deliberate absenteeism can cause many problems to those who are guilty of it. (As a rule, deliberate and frequent absenteeism tends not to be a severe problem in most Infant schools/departments/first schools but it could be worthwhile if the message finds its mark even as early as this. Preface your remarks with: No names, please.)

It is a sad fact of school life that children often stay away from school without a good reason (it need not be your school).

Starters

Why is it bad to miss school when there is no good reason for it?

What might happen to children who deliberately stay away from school?

Story

Mizzy has a Day Off

'Now can you show us what you learnt in the last lesson about Useful Spells?' said the Chief Magician at the School for Young Magicians. Mizzy knew whom he would choose to answer and wished he hadn't skipped school last Monday to go fishing. He hadn't caught anything, anyway.

'Ah, Mizzy,' said the Chief Magician, with a nasty grin, 'Come and cast Spell 66 for us. You do remember how to do it, don't you?'

Mizzy had no idea what Spell 66 was. His friend Lizzy whispered in his ear, 'It was the spell for magicking a coat.'

'Oh, yes, Sir, Chief Magician, the ...er... spell for magicking a coat. Does it matter what kind of coat? A fur coat? A rain coat? Or will any kind of coat be all right?'

The Chief Magician raised one of his bushy eyebrows and said, 'Any kind of coat will do. But be quick. We are all waiting, aren't we, class?' The rest of the young Magicians sniggered and nudged one another. This would be fun. Slowly, Mizzy made his way to the Spell Practice Bench where the Chief Magician gave him a jar of white powder, a tin of treacle and a big bowl.

'Come along now, put the powder and treacle in the bowl and stir. As I showed you,' said the Chief Magician. 'Then say the spell three times as you stir. You do remember the spell, don't you, Mizzy?'

Mizzy tipped the powder and the treacle into the bowl and began to stir the mixture.

'Er... stir the ...er...' he mumbled. The Chief Magician sighed. 'Oh, come along, boy,' he snapped, 'stir the mixture, see it float ...go on ...go on... ' Mizzy went on, 'Stir this mixture, see it float. ...er...'

The Chief Magician was beginning to lose his temper. He said loudly, 'Looks like gravy. Out comes a coat! Say it, then wave your Magic Wand three times and stand back.'

Mizzy was so mixed up that he said, 'Looks like a coat, out comes gravy.' There was a huge bang and the classroom was filled with green smoke. Mizzy found that he was sitting on the floor while a strange creature was eating his hat.

It was a large, pink billy-goat with huge horns. Mizzy had magicked a *goat* instead of a *coat*! He rushed out of the classroom yelling. The goat chased Mizzy up the road, butting him hard every time it caught up with him.

He only escaped by hiding in his Dad's garden shed. The goat ate a row of onions and left after butting the shed door a few times.

Next morning Mizzy was the joke of the school. By the end of the day, he had made up his mind never to skip school again; because, those that skip school always miss learning something important. And he never did.

Songs

Let's pretend	*Tinderbox* 25
Mysteries	*Tinderbox* 40
New things to do	*Tinderbox* 58

A thought to share

If you stay away from school you may never know what you are missing.

Are you listening, God?

Father, we thank you for the chance of going to school.

Thank you, God, for our school and the chance to learn useful and exciting things.

Lord, bless our school and all who teach and learn here.

11 It's better to ask your teacher

Theme

Asking for help

Aim

Encouraging children to bring problems, academic or otherwise, to their teachers.

Starters

What should children do if they were given a sum to do and they found it too hard?
  Should children run to teacher as soon as they get stuck?
  What should they do?

Summing up

We (teachers) are in school for the sole purpose of teaching children; if a child is experiencing difficulty, after making a proper effort they should consult the person who knows.

Story

Jubbly and a Problem

'What *is* the matter with you, Jubbly?' said Mrs Wiseoldbird, the teacher at Wicklepick School for Little Persons. Jubbly had been grumbling to himself ever since the maths lesson had started.

'Nothing, Miss,' he said, pretending to write. It was no good. He could not do this silly take-away sum. But he was not going to ask *her*.

'Add on ten, take away seven,' he muttered. 'Oh, green toadstools and toffee, that's not right.'

Mrs Wiseoldbird pretended not to take any notice and went on listening to Bluebell Bimple's reading. Jubbly tapped Glombo Ploptop on the shoulder.

'Hey, Glommy, what's the answer to Number Six?' he hissed.

'Work it out yourself,' said Glombo, 'or go and ask Miss how to do it.'

'Huh. Not likely. She'll only moan at me,' said Jubbly. He leaned over to Foxglove Flimpat and whispered, 'What's the answer to Number Six, Foxglove?'

Foxglove slammed her book shut and turned her back on him. 'I'm not telling you, Jubbly Jigger. Go and ask teacher how to do it. *She's* the one to ask.' Jubbly growled and went back to his own book. He chewed his pencil as he made an even bigger mess in his book.

Jubbly dropped his pencil on the floor and crept up the gangway to where Toppie Timley, the clever one of the class, was hard at work.

She jumped when Jubbly tugged at her sock and muttered, 'Hey, Brains, what's the answer to Number Six?'

Toppie sniffed and whispered down to Jubbly, 'Go and ask teacher, you stupid boy. That's what she's there for.'

Jubbly groaned and crawled back to his seat. He was just going to slip into the seat when he saw that someone was sitting there already. Without looking up, he poked the person who was sitting in his place and said, through his teeth, 'Oi, get out of my seat before Wiseoldbird sees you there and finds out it isn't me.' Then he looked up. It was his teacher.

'Had a nice crawl, Jubbly?' she said, smiling sweetly. 'Do you really think I don't know what you have been up to? You silly boy, *I* am the one to help you if there is something you can't understand.'

And when she made it seem all so easy, after school, Jubbly decided that she was right, after all.

Songs

Both sides now	*Alleluya* 33
Let's pretend	*Tinderbox* 25
Why does it have to be me?	*Tinderbox* 53

A thought to share

Let us tell ourselves that our teachers are here to help us.

Are you listening, God?

Father God, we know that we can always talk to you.

Dear God, we shall have this day only once; help us not to waste it.

Thank you, Lord, for our teachers and all those who help us.

12 All bullies are cowards

Theme

Bullying

Aim

To bring attention to the subject of bullying and to ascertain children's views about the subject, without involving personalities, victims or perpetrators.

Bullying is a difficult topic, especially with children in this age group. It is, sadly, becoming more prevalent as undesirable behaviour is often copied from older children. Preface any remarks with – No names, please.

Starters

Has anyone been threatened by another child, in school or in other circumstances?

Has anyone ever done any threatening themselves? (you might get some takers...)

Summing up

Let the children come out with the word 'bully' before you do – someone will. Point out that bullies are cowards who only pick on children who they think are weaker than they are.

Suggest that it is not 'telling tales' to complain to a teacher or another responsible adult about bullying. This can be bullying in or out of school and is often the only way to stop the practice.

Story

Preston and the Bow-Wow

Amy and Thomas often take Amy's little sister Katie to play on the swings in the park. One day, they were playing there when who should come along but Preston Stoopey. Preston is a big boy, older than Amy and Thomas and is often, I am sorry to tell you, unkind to smaller children.

Katie was having a lovely swing while Amy and Thomas were swinging on two big rubber tyres. Then they heard Katie screaming. Preston was pushing her swing so high that she was frightened.

'Leave her alone!' shouted Amy, and ran at Preston. He laughed and pushed her into a puddle. Thomas went up to Preston and told him to leave the little girls alone. Preston pushed Thomas really hard and he fell over a little brown dog that was trotting by just at that moment. And the dog bit him – on his bottom.

Thomas ran away, holding his bottom and the dog ran after him, snapping and yapping while Preston stood and cheered and clapped.

'What's the matter, Tom-tom, don't you like bow-wows, then? Ho, ho, ho, ho! Tom-tom doesn't like bow-wows!'

Then a little voice behind him said, 'I'm glad you like bow-wows, Preston. Go on, give Montgomery a pat, then. He seems to like you.' A little old lady, dressed all in green and carrying a large yellow umbrella and a big red bag, was standing next to the biggest dog with the biggest teeth and the longest, pinkest tongue that Preston had ever seen in his life!

'Hello,' said the gigantic dog, only it sounded more like *'Grrrowwwlll!'*

Preston did not wait to see how friendly Montgomery was. He was up a tree before you could say 'Bones and biscuits.'

Montgomery was such a friendly dog that he kept Preston company all night, sitting at the foot of the tree. The little old lady had disappeared and Amy, Thomas and Katie had gone home, so Preston could not ask anyone to rescue him.

The sun was just rising the next morning when Preston realised that the dog had gone. He was so cold that he fell out of the tree and broke his leg and had to be taken to hospital. What a pity.

As he lay in his bed, Preston decided that there was no real fun in bullying children who are smaller or younger or weaker than you are. Because there is always someone else who is bigger than *you* are.

Songs

How do you feel today?	*Play School Songbook* 1
Lord, I love to stamp and shout	*Someone's Singing, Lord* 5
Small is beautiful to be	*Play School Songbook* 22

A thought to share

Although bullies make other people afraid, they are always afraid of something themselves.

Are you listening, God?

Father God, when we are afraid, help us to remember that you are always near to watch over us.

Dear Lord, bless our school and make it a place where we can feel safe and happy.

Father, make us brave enough to tell a grown-up when we are being bullied.

13 A good reason is better than an excuse

Theme

Making excuses

Aim

Persuading children that they do not need an excuse every time they make a mistake.

What would be said if an important message had not been taken home?
   Would teacher be told the truth?
   Which would be the better course of action? Why?

Summing up

Reasons tend to be believed more than excuses and can usually be validated.

Story

Herbert has Another Excuse

'Now read that sentence out to the class, Herbert,' said Mrs Fuzzback. Herbert jumped – he had not heard one word that the teacher had said. He had been thinking about going to pick blackberries after school.

'Well?' said Mrs Fuzzback, 'I'm waiting. And so are the rest of the class.' She was tapping the desk which was always a sign that she was annoyed.

'I ...er... had a bad headache while you were telling us about it, Miss,' he said.

'You've always got an excuse, Herbert,' she said. 'One of these days you will give me a good reason instead.'

Herbert was not sorry when the bell rang for home time but he was in such a hurry to get out that he forgot his homework book.

When he got home, his mother called from the kitchen, 'Did you bring that sugar from the shop on the way home?' Herbert wiggled his little black snout. He had forgotten, as usual.

'Oh ...I...er... I didn't take any money this morning,' he said.

'Yes, you did,' said his mother, 'I saw you put it in your lunch box.' She opened it and there was the money.

'Oh ...I...er... I·had to go and count the sticks of chalk for Mrs. Fuzzback,' said Herbert.

'Oh, yes,' said his mother, 'and how many were there?' Herbert did not expect that. He spluttered into the nettle pop he was drinking.

'Oh...ar...I couldn't reach the shelf where it's kept,' he gasped, 'so she told me to go home.'

Next morning, after assembly, Mrs Fuzzback said, 'Now hedgehogs, do you remember that I told you to ask your parents what a hedgehog should do if you find yourself in danger from bad animals like foxes, who enjoy a nice juicy hedgehog for their dinner? Stand up and tell us, Herbert.'

But Herbert had forgotten to ask his parents. Teacher made him stay in at playtime and write, 'All hedgehogs roll into a ball if a fox tries to bite them.'

He never forgot it, especially one day when Silas Slink, a very foxy gentleman, fancied young hedgehog for lunch. But all he got was a snout full of prickles; and Herbert realised that making excuses all the time is very silly because you were bound to get caught some time.

It was just as well he did get caught, or he wouldn't be here to tell me the tale I have just told you.

Songs

Can anyone tell me that?	*Tinderbox* 6
Mysteries	*Tinderbox* 40
Turn, turn, turn	*Alleluya* 32

A thought to share

It is best to own up when you have made a mistake and not to make poor excuses.

Are you listening, God?

Father, help us to be honest when we have not done something we should have done.

Father, help us, too, when we have done something that we should not have done.

Father God, help us to understand that making excuses is usually a waste of everybody's time.

14 Listening is not the same as hearing

Theme

Listening (1)

Aim:

Stressing the importance of listening properly, in and out of school.

Starters

Say any string of non-sequential numbers.

Ask if anyone can repeat the string exactly. There will not be many successes.

Summing up

Even if we try hard we cannot listen properly for very long. Children listen even less effectively than adults. Individuals have no control over this. At the same time it is possible for most people, including children, to listen carefully enough to remember information, such as instructions. When teacher says, 'Listen carefully' then this should be a signal for doing just that.

Story

Jubbly and the Angry Porker

Jubbly never listens properly to *anything* he is supposed to. He says he can't help it, but his teacher, Mrs Wiseoldbird, thinks he could at least try.

One day, he was told to put the class books away after a writing lesson. Jubbly threw them away into the bin, so perhaps you see what I mean.

He is just as bad at home. Once his mother told him to fetch the honey for her toast. Jubbly put her purse on the table because he thought she had said 'money'.

If anyone sends him to the shop on an errand, he usually comes back with the wrong things. Aunt Letitia Burble sent him to buy a stick of French bread and he bought her a pot of French mustard. Great Aunt Dandelion sent him to buy her a cheese-and-tomato pizza and he came back with a lump of cheese, six tomatoes and a tin of chicken soup.

Uncle Grizzle Hockweed asked him to collect the medicine for his bad leg from the chemist and please would he hurry. Jubbly came back with a hot curry from Noknok's Indian Take-away. Uncle Grizzle chased him down the road, even with his bad leg.

One day Jubbly went to pick strawberries. At the end of the day, Farmer Cornstraw gave him five pounds and a basket of strawberries, and said, 'Well done'. Then he told Jubbly to make sure that he did *not* go home through the *pig* meadow. But was Jubbly listening?

He went into a lovely green meadow which seemed all right. No, it was not a *big* meadow – that was what Farmer Cornstraw had said, wasn't it?

Then he heard a very alarming noise. It was not exactly a squeal. It was not exactly a roar. But, when he turned round, Jubbly saw the fiercest porker he had ever seen – a huge, hairy pig called Boomer. He charged at Jubbly, who scrambled up the nearest tree, quicker than you can say 'Trotters and Tails'.

Jubbly spent the night up the tree, not knowing that Boomer had gone back to his sty. By the morning he was very sore and stiff and he felt sick after eating all the strawberries that the farmer had given him.

His parents were so worried because they couldn't find him – they even called out PC Poppletip to look for Jubbly but he couldn't find him, either – and he was not very pleased at missing a night's sleep.

Jubbly got a terrible telling-off; and he was not allowed to spend his five pounds but had to put it in the bank.

Since then, Jubbly tries very hard to listen carefully when someone is telling him something. Mind you, he doesn't always get it right even now.

Songs

Can you hear?	*Harlequin* 33
Do your ears hang low?	*Okki-tokki-unga* 25
Sound song	*Tinderbox* 39

A thought to share

Anybody can hear but not everybody can listen properly.

Are you listening, God?

Father God, help us to know the difference between listening and just hearing.

Father of us all, we know you are listening to us when we speak to you.

Teach us, Father, when to speak and when to listen.

15 How carefully were you listening?

Theme

Listening (2)

Aim

To encourage discriminating listening. Not to be taken too seriously, but is a useful follow-up from the previous assembly.

Who can pick out the word that is different from the others?

red blue fat yellow green	(fat)
boy girl man rabbit woman	(rabbit)
pizza sausage burger cabbage	(cabbage)
dog horse cat sparrow	(sparrow)

(Can be followed up in classroom)

Summing up

There are times when extra attention must be paid because someone is saying something important.

(You could spend some classroom time talking about 'Dutch auctions' at street markets, where it is very important to listen to what the traders are saying.)

Story

The Smart Squirrel

'I told you they were here,' said Spike Squirrel. 'That was a bit of luck.'

'I thought we'd never find them,' said his cousin Sonia.

The squirrels had found the hoard of nuts that they had hidden before the snows came. Spike bit into one.

'Perfect,' he said, smacking his lips.

'Well, share them out,' said Sonia. 'Don't just sit there munching away.'

'All right,' said Spike, reaching into the hole in the old tree and pulling out more of the shiny brown nuts. 'One for you, one for me,' he said, putting a nut on the ground in front of Sonia and one in front of hinself. She rubbed her paws together. This was exciting!

'Two for you; one, two for me,' said Spike. He put another nut in front of Sonia and counted out two more in front of himself. Sonia stopped rubbing her paws.

Spike went on, 'Three for you; one, two, three for me.' He put one more nut in front of his cousin and counted out three more for himself. Sonia had a puzzled look on her face. Somehow, Spike's pile looked bigger than hers.

Spike grinned as he went on counting, 'Four for you; one, two, three, four for me.' He put another nut on the ground in front of Sonia and counted out four more for himself.

'Hey, cousin,' said Sonia, swishing her bushy tail, 'what are you up to? You've got …um… all those. But I've only got four nuts.'

Spike's grin grew even bigger. 'I've been sharing them out, haven't I? Look, I'll show you.' He put one nut down with Sonia's share and said, 'There, that's five for you.' Then he counted out nuts on to his pile. 'One, two, three, four, five for me.'

'You cheeky thing,' said Sonia, 'you may be sharing out the nuts. But that's not sharing them out *fairly*. You've got… you've got… um

...ever such a lot. I've only got ... five. That's not fair.'

Spike burst out laughing. 'Of course not, you soppy squirrel,' he said. 'I wondered how long it would be before you spotted what I was up to! You should listen *properly* to something important.' Then he shared them out, fairly this time.

I'm sure you spotted what Spike was doing long before Sonia Squirrel did.

And have you worked out how many nuts he had before Sonia realised he was playing a trick on her?

Songs

If you're happy	*Apusskidu* 1
Try again	*Tinderbox* 56
Turn, turn, turn	*Alleluya* 32

A thought to share

Not listening properly is as bad as not listening at all.

Are you listening, God?

Father, we thank you for the gift of hearing.

Please, Father God, give us the patience to listen carefully to other people.

Father of us all, help us to do the things we should and be to others kind and good.

16 Don't be late!

Theme

Punctuality

Aim

Illustrating the virtues and benefits of punctuality.

Starters

Why is it important to be able to tell the time?
  Who can tell the time?
  What are the disadvantages of not being able to tell the time?
  What problems can be caused by persistent unpunctuality?
  What are the causes of unpunctuality? Are they remediable?
  Should persistent unpunctuality be a punishable offence in your
school? (it may already be so ...)

Summing up

Don't always rely on adults/others and learn to tell the time as soon as
possible.

Poem

The Sad Tale of Lollipop, who wanted to be a Rock and Roll Singer

Lollipop loved rock and roll,
To be a singer was her goal.
She longed for fortune and for fame
When everyone would know her name.
But she would never be so famous.
Her parents said, 'You musn't blame us.
Our stupid daughter's always late
And misses such important dates.
We do not know what we can do...
On keeping time she has no clue.'
They bought her watches, chiming clocks
And loud alarms packed in a box;
But Lollipop had no idea
That this of course would cost her dear.
Because one day she had to go
And practise for a music show.

Her mother said, 'You'll miss the bus!'
But daughter said, 'Oh, please don't fuss.
I do not think you have to worry,
There is no need for me to hurry.'
But Lollipop arrived too late,
She got herself in such a state.
The doorman said, 'There's no one 'ere,
The show is over till next year.'
She kicked and battered at the door.
She screamed and rolled upon the floor.
It did no good, police were brought,
And Lollipop was sent to court.
The magistrate said, 'Go to jail!'
The girl let out a dreadful wail.
That was the end of her big chance
To sing upon the stage, or dance.
She now works in a record store
Sells tapes and videos and much more;
She'll never be a star of rock
Because she didn't see the clock.

Songs

I jump out of bed in the morning	*Okki-tokki-unga* 47
Morning has broken	*Someone's Singing, Lord* 3
Sun arise	*Tinderbox* 43

A thought to share

Ask yourself whether it is better to arrive late than not at all.

Are you listening, God?

Father God, do not allow us to waste this day or any other day.

Thank you, Lord, for every hour of the day and night.

Dear God, we ask you to help us to spend our time in useful ways.

17 Rules are made to help everyone

Theme

School rules

Aim

To help children understand that all societies need a framework of reasonable order.

Starters

Does your school have school rules?
    Are they written down?
    If yes, what do they mean (rule by rule)?
    If not, what rules are children expected to obey?
    In both cases, why do we need rules?

Summing up

The children's ideas on sanctions for miscreants in both situations are often interesting...

Story

Jubbly and the School Rules

Jubbly saw a large piece of paper which he had never seen before, on the classroom wall. As he is a nosey sort of Little Person, Jubbly had a good look at it before his teacher Mrs Wiseoldbird came into mark the register.

He did not like what he saw. He read, 'Wicklepick School Rules'. There were only two rules and they were simple.

Rule One said, 'Things that could hurt other children should be left at home.'

Rule Two said, 'Things that cost a lot of money should be left at home.'

'Hey, Bunjy,' he said to his best friend, 'have you seen these rules? What do we want them for?'

Before Bunjy could answer, teacher came into the room and said, 'Good morning, children,' and 'Sit down, Jubbly.'

'Miss,' said Jubbly, 'why do we need School Rules? I think they're stupid.'

Mrs Wiseoldbird said smiling, 'If you don't know, Jubbly, then you must find out for yourself. I'm not going to tell you.'

At playtime Jubbly was still moaning about it. Bunjy was just about to tell him to shut up when they heard a terrific din in the middle of the playground. Jubbly's cousin, Tinsel Jellybit, was screeching at Daisy Dimpletoe and holding what was left of a pretty necklace.

'You've broken my necklace, you silly girl! I told you to look at it, not try it on. Now look what you've done!' she screamed, her face a bright red colour.

All the children were soon rushing about the playground, picking up the shiny beads that had made Tinsel's birthday necklace. A lot of them went down a drain and Tinsel's necklace would never be the same again. It had cost a lot of money, too and her mother had told her she was not to take it to school. But she had.

Then there was another lot of noise from under the conker tree in the corner of the playground. Cracker Spottle was roaring and holding his eye. Bomble Woblot was fussing round him, telling everybody that he hadn't *meant* to let the conker fly from his catapult and hit Cracker in the eye.

'It was an accident, Cracker, honest,' he wailed. Cracker had to go home and be taken to see Doctor Plong. He had to wear a bandage for a whole week.

After that, Jubbly knew that some rules are needed in a school and there was no need for him to ask Mrs Wiseoldbird to explain why.

Songs

If you're happy and you know it   *Apusskidu* 1
Join in the game   *Okki Tokki Unga* 2
The world is big, the world is small   *Tinderbox* 33

A thought to share

Think quietly – If there were no fools we would not need rules.

Are you listening, God?

Father God, help us to understand why we need some rules in our school.

Father, teach us to care about other people.

Father God, teach us to grow up so that we do not need too many rules.

18 Sticks and stones

Theme

Teasing

Aim

To explain that teasing is an undesirable and hurtful form of behaviour.

Starters

Ensure no names are used.

How well-known is the saying, 'Sticks and stones may break my bones but names will never hurt me'?

What does it mean?

Is it true?

What do people get teased about? (appearance, stature, clothing, disability, accent etc.)

How can it be stopped in our school or outside?

Summing up

It can be difficult to persuade children to be sensible and constructive about stopping teasing, but it is worth persevering. Teasing is a form of bullying, and that should never be tolerated.

Story

The Ugly Chicken

Once there was a brood of seven chickens. Six of them were covered with fluffy, yellow down and were very pretty.

But one little chicken, whose down was a dull brown colour, was not pretty like his brothers and sisters. The other chickens teased him and called him cruel names, like 'Mucky' and 'Muddy' and teased him so much that he often hid in the haystack and cried. Even Mrs Hen thought he was ugly.

'You're not a bit like your brothers and sisters,' she said. 'I can't imagine how your egg got in my nest. To think I actually hatched you out. You are the ugliest chicken I have ever seen.'

As the pretty chickens grew, they teased him even more and called him even worse names, like 'Uggy Muggy' and 'Pudding Beak'. The poor little chicken hid in dark corners of the barn and sobbed because the teasing was so cruel. When he came out for dinner, he begged the other chickens not to call him names because he could not help being ugly.

But all they did was to steal his share of corn and scratch dust into his face.

Then, one day, they decided to drive their ugly brother out of the farmyard. They chased him out into the meadow, cackling and squawking and calling him more names like 'Dirty Duck' and 'Scraggy Neck'. The poor chicken did not know what to do or where to go.

So he started walking. After walking for days he found himself in a huge garden. As he squeezed through a hedge he bumped into the most beautiful creature he had ever seen. It had a deep blue neck, green wings and a marvellous long tail, covered in big spots that looked like a lot of eyes. On its head was a crest, just like a crown.

'Hello,' said the beautiful bird. 'We don't often see a strange young peacock here.'

'Me?' said the ugly chicken. 'I'm a chicken, not a whatever-you-called-it.'

'No,' said the beautiful bird, 'you are not a chicken. You are a peacock. You may not look like me now but, one day soon, you will look just like me.'

Sure enough, in a few weeks' time, the ugly chicken did – only even more beautiful.

Songs

Both sides now   *Alleluya* 33
He gave me eyes so I could see   *Someone's Singing, Lord* 19
If you're happy   *Apusskidu* 1

A thought to share

May we never be stupid enough to poke fun at another because we may
seem funny to them.

Are you listening, God?

Father, God, let me be kind to all people, big or small.

Dear God, teach me to understand that what I think is ugly may be
beautiful to someone else.

Father, help us to understand that words can hurt people.

All around us

19 There are better places to play

Theme

The dangers lurking on building sites

Aim

Suggesting that children keep away from the potential hazards of building sites.

This assembly is best used near the start of any of the holidays, including half term, and may be supported by a visit from a professional person in the building trade. Children of any age find building sites attractive and hazards cannot be overstated.

Starters

What dangerous things might be found where building work is going on? (The children may be able to tell you, but, if not, the most likely hazards are scaffolding, ladders and stacked bricks/concrete blocks etc.)

Are there any dangers that are not obvious? (stacked bags of cement, sand piles, girders etc.)

What is the best way to avoid the dangers of a building site?

Story

Curtly, Charlie and a Foolish Adventure

Curtly said to his best friend Charlie, 'What shall we do today?'

'I don't know,' said Charlie, 'you choose.'

'OK,' said Curtly, 'let's go and watch them building those new flats up at Holly Avenue.'

Charlie thought this was a good idea, and off they went. To their surprise, nobody was working there.

'Let's explore,' said Curtly.

Charlie said, 'My Mum would kill me if she knew. She's always telling me to stay away from places that could be dangerous.'

'You're scared,' scoffed Curtly. 'Scared of what your Mummy will say. Anyway, how will she find out? I won't tell if you don't.' He pushed his friend into a pile of sand and ran up a ladder that stood against a wooden platform about fifteen metres high above the ground. The platform, made from wooden planks fixed to steel poles, is called scaffolding. Builders stand on it when they have to work high up.

Curtly danced along the platform making silly noises and faces. The planks swayed and bounced up and down as he danced. Then, suddenly, they gave way. There was a loud crash. Curtly fell off the platform, yelling as he fell.

He came to a stop about ten metres up from the ground. His tee-shirt had caught on the end of a scaffold pole and the frightened boy dangled there, his eyes rolling. Charlie could hear his shirt tearing, very, very slowly. But it was better than crashing on to the concrete-mixer that was on the muddy ground below.

Just then Charlie heard someone shouting, 'Oi! You kids, what do you think you're doing? Get out of it!' A big security guard was waving his arms at Charlie. Behind him was a very large German shepherd dog.

Charlie was too frightened to move, and Curtly couldn't. Then the guard saw Curtly and began to laugh. He asked some men who were passing by to help him get Curtly down from the pole. They did it just as his shirt gave way.

When he was safe on the ground, do you know what the guard did? No, he did not ask Curtly if he was all right or offer to take him home. He told the dog to chase the boys off the building site. It did, too.

You will not be surprised to know that Curtly and Charlie never went on to a building site again. As Charlie said, 'Building sites are too dangerous to be a playground.'

Songs

Can anyone tell me that?	*Tinderbox* 6
New things to do	*Tinderbox* 58
With a little help from my friends	*Alleluya* 38

A thought to share

May we remember that if we put ourselves in danger we may put someone else in danger, too.

Are you listening, God?

Father God, keep us safe from harm when we are foolish and do stupid things.

Please, God, help us to know what are sensible games and what are not.

Dear God, we shall have this day only once. Help us not to waste it.

20 How safe is the countryside?

Theme

Danger in the countryside

Aim

Bringing to children's attention the fact that unexpected dangers exist in the rural environment just as much as in towns.

Your approach to this topic will, obviously, vary according to the school environment. Most children in rural areas are already aware of the dangers that lurk on farms but they should still be reminded of them. Urban children should also learn something about the hazards of the countryside. With the increasing popularity of farms that include 'Visitor's Centres', the topic may well have more relevance than it had a few years ago. Most children will have some idea of risks in the countryside from TV and other publicity.

Starters

What dangers might be found on a farm?

　Are there any dangers that may not be obvious?

　What is the best way to avoid the dangers to be found on a farm?

Story

Wilfred, Flossie and a Narrow Escape

'And where do you think you are going, young man?' said Mrs Flopears.

Young Wilfred twitched his nose and said, 'Only up to Hazel Corner to play with Flossie Fuzztail.'

'Well, that's all right, then,' said Mum. 'So long as you don't go near Willow Farm. Remember, it's not safe, with those nasty tractors and things. Very bad for rabbit children. Or any other children, for that matter.'

But Wilfred was more interested in what Farmer Cropper had unloaded into his barn two days earlier.

Wilfred said to himself, as he ran up the road to meet his friend, 'I wonder if it's carrots? Or perhaps it's lettuces?' Silly Wilfred - farmers never store things like that in a barn!

When he and Flossie got to the farm, they made sure that Rosie, the terrier, was not about, because she did not like rabbits.

A door was open at the back of the barn and the rabbits climbed the ladder standing there. They found they were standing on a wide ledge, looking down at – not carrots, nor lettuces, but what looked like a big yellow pond. The barn was full of corn, the sort used to make cornflakes.

'I don't like corn,' said Wilfred and Flossie together. They turned to go home and – Flossie slipped. She fell, with a rabbit scream, into the corn. Wilfred tried to grab her and he fell in, too. They started to struggle and they began to sink, because corn moves about like soft sand.

The more they struggled, the faster they sank. Then, just as they were about to disappear two big hands grabbed their ears, one pair of ears in each hand.

'What have we got here, then?' boomed a human voice.

'Couple of rabbits, Ted,' said another human voice.

'Oh, I do like a nice bit o' pie,' said the first voice.

As soon as Wilfred and Flossie heard the word 'pie', they wriggled and squiggled – and dragged their ears out of the big hands.

They were back in Chomper Village quicker than you could, say, 'Potatoes and gravy'! And they never went near Willow Farm again.

Songs

Can anyone tell me that?	*Tinderbox* 6
I whistle a happy tune	*Apusskidu* 3
Turn, turn, turn	*Alleluya* 32

A thought to share

We must never forget that anyone who takes silly risks is asking for trouble.

Are you listening, God?

Father, help us to enjoy our countryside but teach us to be careful, too.

Father God, we thank you for the open air and for the fun that summertime can bring.

Dear God, thank you for farms and farmers and for our food.

21 Flowers or vegetables?

Theme

Gardens

Aim

To encourage children to appreciate that flowers and vegetables are equally important.

Starters

Name some flowers.
    Do they have a scent?
    What colour are they?
    Name some vegetables.
    Do they grow above ground or below?
    (Follow up at classroom level.)

Story

The Arguing Neighbours

'Morning, Belinda,' said Thrush to Blackbird. 'Lovely day. I see that Mr Croppit and Mrs Cheerie are arguing again.' She pointed a wing at the neighbours who had just come out into their gardens.

'Oh, slugs,' Mr Croppit was growling. 'They've had a lovely feast off my beans.'

'You'll have to put down some slug pellets, Mr Croppit. Or they'll eat the lot,' said Mrs Cheerie over the fence. 'Yes, I will,' grunted Mr Croppit.

Mrs. Cheerie wagged a finger at him and said, 'You make sure you put down the kind of pellets that don't harm the hedgehogs and birds.' Croppit leaned on his spade and said, 'Oh, they cost much more than ordinary pellets.'

'Yes, just a little,' said his neighbour, 'But we must look after our garden friends, you know. And don't forget to put some round the flowers, too.'

'Flowers? Flowers? You know I don't waste my time growing flowers!' said Croppit, his face turning red. 'You can't eat flowers! If you can't eat them, don't grow them, that's what I always say!'

'Oh, you miserable man!' said Mrs Cheerie. 'What a drab and gloomy world it would be without any flowers. You can't put brussels sprouts in a vase. Or do flower arrangements with lettuces and leeks.'

'Huh,' snorted Croppit, 'And you can't eat boiled daffodils, either, because they are poisonous.'

'Do you mean to say, Henry Croppit, that if you had your way, people wouldn't grow pansies or petunias or primroses?' said Charlotte.

'Vegetables are just as handsome as flowers,' grunted Mr Croppit. 'Think of the lovely red colour of beetroot and dark green of a nice cabbage.'

'Oh, dear,' sighed Theodore Thrush, 'they'll never learn, will they? Can't someone tell them that we need flowers *and* vegetables? Otherwise it would be a very strange world.'

And so it would.

Songs

Let it be	*Tinderbox* 48
One potato, two potato	*Apusskidu* 31
Think of a world without any flowers	*Someone's Singing, Lord* 15

A thought to share

Think about how beautiful flowers are but think, too, about the taste of vegetables.

Are you listening, God?

Thank you, Lord, for the happiness that flowers bring to people.

Dear God, show us what is beautiful and what is good.

Thank you, Father, for all good things that grow in gardens and on farms.

22　Why *do* people write on walls?

Theme

Graffiti

Aim

Suggesting to children that there are better things to write on than walls, and that those who deface walls are anti-social people.

As with most unsocial behaviour, children of early years tend to ape their seniors and to copy their behaviour – graffiti is no exception. The infant/first stage of education is not too early to look at this topic.

Starters

Who has seen writing/drawings on places where such adornment is obviously not meant to be?
    Where?
    Who does it?
    Why do they do it?
    Has anyone here ever done it? (an optimistic enquiry...)
    Can we do anything about it?
    What if it happens in school?

Story

Jubbly and a Felt Pen

It all began when Great Aunt Dandelion gave Jubbly a red felt pen. She should really have known better.

Aunt Myrtle Spottle, who keeps the village shop, had given him a roll of wallpaper and he enjoyed drawing grubs and bugs and butterflies on that. He wrote his name thirty times and his two-times table six times. Then Jubbly got tired of drawing and writing on a roll of wallpaper and thought, 'I must show everyone what a clever Little Person I am!'

He rushed out of the cottage and wrote, on the nearest tree, 'Jubbly is King!' He knew he wasn't a king but it looked exciting. He trotted up the High Street and wrote it again on Mayor Oompah's front door – twice.

He drew a ten-legged bug on the window of Greengrocer Nutlark's shop, and got chased up the road. He squiggled on Mr Timble's milk cart, drew a butterfly on Antonio Flucci's ice-cream van, and wrote his name on old Snorter, the baker's horse, who was asleep at the time.

Altogether, he made a dreadful mess all over Wicklepick. He had just finished writing his name (again) on the village lamp-post when who should come along but Aunt Eliza Jellybit.

Nobody upsets Aunt Eliza Jellybit, and Jubbly soon found out why. She took hold of Jubbly's long left ear (Little People's ears are not like ours – they are rather pointed at the top and bottom) between her long, rough fingers and dragged him to her cottage.

There she gave Jubbly a bucket of hot water, a scrubbing brush and a bar of hard, green soap. She made him go all round the village scrubbing off his scribblings. He was unable to get it off the first time and he had to scrub each scribble four times before Aunt Eliza was satisfied. As she told him when she watched him emptying the water away, 'Other people don't wish to see your silly scribblings, especially when you have done them in places where they should not be. If you want to draw and write, do them on the proper thing – paper. Then nobody will be annoyed. Least of all, me.'

Songs

New things to do	*Tinderbox* 58
Sing a song of people	*Tinderbox* 18
The Tidy Song	*Tinderbox* 47

A thought to share

Think before you write or draw in places where nobody wants to see how clever you are.

Are you listening, God?

Thank you, Lord, for your wonderful world. May we do nothing to spoil it.

Father, teach us to not to spoil our towns and villages.

Thank you, Father, for the people who keep our towns and villages clean.

23 Pick it up!

Theme

Litter

Aim

Encouraging children not to drop litter and, if they see litter, to pick it up and put it in the bin.

Starters

What *is* litter?
    What kind of litter is most common?
    Where does litter come from? Why?
    What can be do about it – in school, at home?

Story

Jasper and the Litter

Jasper is a very well-behaved boy. He is seven years old, very kind and helpful and his manners are very good. He never eats with his mouth open, never picks up chips with his fingers and most certainly never sticks his fork into a sausage so that he can bite chunks off it.

Jasper never fails to say 'Please' and 'Thank you' at parties, goes to bed without grumbling and *never* has to be told to wash his hands. But Jasper was not always as good as this. Oh, dear, no. Jasper, I am sorry to tell you, dropped... litter.

Crisp-packets, lolly-wrappers, sweet-papers, burger-packs, hot-dog napkins, drink-cans and cartons, orange-peel, banana-skins – it did not matter what it was. After he had unwrapped, opened or unpeeled – he threw the rubbish straight on to the ground, wherever he was. What was worse, he did not seem to care at all.

Until, one day, Jasper was in the school playground, eating a chocolate biscuit from his lunch. He unwrapped the biscuit – and can you guess what he did with the paper? Yes, he threw it on the ground.

Then to his surprise, he saw a strange little old lady, dressed from head to foot in green, carrying a large yellow umbrella and a big red bag. She walked across the playground and stood in front of him.

She said in a squeaky little voice, 'Hello, Jasper. I think it is time you should see what might happen if you do not put your litter into a bin.'

Before Jasper could say a word, the little old lady pointed the yellow umbrella at him. There was a sudden rush of wind. The wrapper that he had thrown on to the ground leapt up and whirled round and round his head, so that he felt quite dizzy.

Then the wrapper became two wrappers, and three, and four, and five – and soon Jasper could see nothing but a spinning storm of wrappers. They seemed to pile up all round him. Soon he was buried up to his neck in biscuit wrappers. Jasper was terrified. Then, just as suddenly, they vanished. All that was left was one blue wrapper being blown round his feet.

Jasper heard a little, squeaky voice from behind him. 'Do you see what I mean?' it said. He turned round but there was no one to be seen. Straight away, Jasper picked up the wrapper and rushed with it to the nearest litter bin. And, ever since he saw the strange little old lady, he has never dropped litter again – anywhere.

Songs

I would like to be	*Tinderbox* 45
Milk bottle tops and paper bags	*Someone's singing, Lord* 17
The tidy song	*Tinderbox* 47

A thought to share

If nobody drops litter there will be none to pick up.

Are you listening, God?

Father, teach us to keep our streets and countryside clean.

Dear Father God, help us to look after the places where we live.

Dear God, make us sensible and caring children.

24 Everyone should learn to swim

Theme

Swimming

Aim of assembly

To encourage all children to avail themselves of any opportunity to learn to swim.

This assembly obviously has no validity where there are no local amenities. It is intended to encourage those children with access to swimming pools to avail themselves of what is on offer.

Starters

Who can swim properly and without swimming aids?
   Who can swim but only do doggy paddle?
   Who can swim with swimming aids?
   Who is learning to swim?
   Where?
   How?
   Who knows the names of some swimming strokes.
   Why should everyone learn to swim?

Poem

The tale of Kim, Who did not Wish to Learn to Swim

A six-year old, whose name was Kim,
Said she would never learn to swim.
She hated smelly swimming-pools
And claimed keen swimmers were all fools.

She thought swimming lessons were a joke,
And would never talk of swimming strokes.
Whether they were breast or crawl,
She really did not care at all.
Now one fine day she took a ride
To picnic at the river-side,
A basket to her cycle tied
With scrummy goodies packed inside.
A beeline for some trees she made,
Hoping she would find some shade.
Arriving there, she pressed her brakes,
But pressed too hard – a big mistake!
The girl went hurtling through the air
And landed – yes, you've guessed just where,
Straight in the water with a plop;
There was no way that Kim could stop.
She struggled in the water deep
And woke a lady fast asleep;
This lady, though aged ninety-two,
Knew exactly what to do.
She threw her shoes aside and dived;
Without her Kim could not survive.
The lady towed her to the bank.
The girl had no breath left to thank
The lady who had dragged her out.
Her life was saved, without a doubt.
When Kim got home, all dripping wet,
She had no time to sit and fret;
Her Mama said 'You'll learn to swim!'
And called a teacher, name of Jim.
He taught the girl to keep afloat
If she should fall out of a boat;
And how she was her breath to hold,

Keep moving if the water's cold.
Soon she was swimming with the best;
Jim taught her backstroke and the rest.
Before the girl had reached sixteen
She'd entered the Olympic scene;
She won three medals made of gold
– And all because that lady old
Had learnt to swim when she was five
And Kim, the champion – stayed alive!

Songs

For all the strength we have	*Someone's Singing, Lord* 16
Hands to work and feet to run	*Someone's Singing, Lord* 21
Messing about on the river	*Jolly Herring* 72

A thought to share

We should do everything we can to learn all we can.

Are you listening, God?

Thank you, Father, for our wonderful bodies.

Father God, help us to do all we can to keep ourselves safe from harm.

Thank you, Lord, for swimming pools and people who teach us how to swim.

25 Don't put it down

Theme

Tidiness

Aim

Encouraging children to have a place for everything at school and, hopefully, at home.

Your younger charges are not likely to take the topic very seriously but Y2/Y3 children should learn that order is an important element of discipline and the overall school image. Everyone, even the youngest children, should understand that there is a place for everything and, without a proper organisation of resources, chaos is never far away.

Starters

Where are the reading books are kept?

How are they identified? (This can be extended/adapted to other types of resource)

What should be done if books etc. are left lying around?

Who should be responsible for replacing resource material?

Story

Put it away

Sara's mother stopped threading her tapestry needle and sighed when she heard a crash and a howl from Sara, who was upstairs.

'I can never find anything in that stupid wardrobe,' wailed Sara, looking round the door. 'Have you seen my ballet shoes?'

Her mother said crossly, 'I've told you a hundred times to put things where you can find them.' Sara rushed back upstairs, talking to herself.

'What's wrong with her?' said her brother Shane. Without waiting for an answer, he said, 'Hey, Mum, seen my football boots?'

His mother shook her head and said, 'Why ask me? You were told to clean them and then put them where you could find them. Did you... ?' She found she was talking to herself – Shane had stamped out of the back door.

'What have you done with the car keys?' said Mr Jones as Shane pushed past him. Mrs Jones put her work down and tried not to lose her temper.

She said, very slowly, 'I have not seen your car keys. Perhaps they have gone to find Sara's ballet shoes which are probably searching for Shane's football boots which are most likely hunting for the watch you couldn't find yesterday. And I wouldn't be surprised if that wasn't out somewhere looking for Sara's best blue leotard that she couldn't find last Saturday. And that's probably trying to find the crash helmet that Shane said he'd lost the Thursday before.'

Mr Jones looked surprised. Before he could say anything Mrs Jones said, 'Things are going to change around here.'

Mr Jones suddenly found that he had the the car keys in his pocket all the time and he left in a hurry.

The next morning, Sara found a sheet of blue paper in the fridge as she got out the milk for her cornflakes. There was another one in her school games bag. Shane found a piece of yellow paper under his toothbrush and another one under his trainers. Mr Jones found a piece of green paper under his newspaper and another one under his brief case on the hall table. On each one was the message in very large letters:

'DON'T PUT IT <u>DOWN</u> – PUT IT <u>AWAY</u> !'

From that time on, they did exactly that. Well, most of the time, anyway. Of course, *you* put things away all the time. Don't you?

Songs

Each day different	*Harlequin* 43
How many people live in your house?	*Tinderbox* 19
One, two, three	*Tinderbox* 65

A thought to share

It is easier to make a mess than it is to clear it up.

Are you listening, God?

Dear Father, show us the best way to help others.

Father God, help us to make the world a cleaner and tidier place.

Dear Lord, teach us to do what we can to help those people who look after us.

26 A strange way to enjoy yourself!

Theme

Vandalism

Aim

To suggest that the destruction of the things around us is a mindless and selfish occupation.

As with graffiti, the youngest children will not always appreciate what you are talking about, but, those at the top of the school/department will be fully aware of the message, and six is not too early an age for this subject.

Starters

Why do people – usually younger people – damage property and the environment for no good reason?

What can be done about vandalism? (Responses to the last question will vary – Y2/Y3 children in some schools may come up with some interesting thoughts. Worth pursuing in the classroom.)

Story

The Foolish Elephants

Boss Tiger was annoyed. The forest looked as if it had been hit by a storm, but there had been no storm. Branches had been torn off the trees and fruit lay squashed and trampled on the ground.

All around were dead, broken flowers and bushes. Ferns had been ripped up and left on the ground. Nearby were three broken eggs which must have come from a parrot's nest.

'I must find out what has happened,' growled Boss Tiger. He came across a troop of monkeys that were chattering and eating bananas.

'Do you know what has happened in the forest?' asked Boss Tiger.

'No,' said Head Monkey. 'We have been asleep all day.' Then Boss Tiger saw some buffalo, on their way to the water-hole.

'Do you know what has happened in the forest?' he asked. 'No,' said Chief Buffalo. 'We have only just arrived.'

Just then, Boss Tiger was pushed out of the way by a young elephant who charged past him, trumpeting and laughing loudly. He was followed by a gang of six young bull elephants and four cow elephants, all making a dreadful noise. They did not seem to care what they broke as they charged past.

'Hoy!' roared Boss Tiger, 'come here!' He stopped the last of the young calves by grabbing its tail. The young elephant came to a sudden stop with a squeal.

'Did you do all that damage in the forest?' roared Boss Tiger, loosening his grip on the elephant's tail. The rest of the young elephants stopped and came back. Nobody argues with Boss Tiger. They looked very ashamed. Sheepish, even, that is if elephants can look like sheep.

The biggest calf swung his trunk, scraped at the ground with his foot and said, 'It was only a bit of fun, Boss Tiger.'

Boss Tiger roared, 'Do you know what you are, you stupid elephants? You are *vandals!*'

'What's a vandal, Mr Boss Tiger, Sir?' asked one of the elephants.

Boss Tiger snarled, ' Vandals are animals that break things just for fun. At least, they think it's fun. If they stopped to think a bit more. they might understand that they are spoiling things for other animals. They might even hurt other animals. But you are just stupid young elephants. Did you know that the worst vandals of all are stupid young – human beings?'

Songs

I would like to be	*Tinderbox* 45
Let it be	*Tinderbox* 48
The angry song	*Tinderbox* 9

A thought to share

Can you imagine what the vandals will do when they have smashed all there is to smash?

Are you listening, God?

Thank you, God, for the good things in this world.

Father, may we do all we can to protect the good things we them against people who break them without a reason.

Lord, help us to make vandals see that they are spoiling our country.

This and that

27 Don't count your chickens

Theme

Making plans too soon

Aim

Re-telling an old story about planning some things too far in advance. This is not an assembly with a 'moral', so don't take it too seriously.

Starters

Who has made plans to do something and the plans have gone wrong? What happened?

Summing up

Planning is important, but not always too far in advance in case things go wrong.

Story

Henrietta and the Eggs

Once upon a time, a poor farmer had a daughter whose name was Henrietta. Although he was poor, her father was very kind to her and bought her pretty ribbons whenever he could afford it. This was because he did not have enough money to buy her a new hat.

One day, he said that for her birthday she could keep the next batch of eggs that his hens laid. Then, on market day, she could sell the chicks that would hatch out.

So, one fine day in June, Henrietta collected twenty-four speckled brown eggs that the hens had laid. As she went to find a hen to sit on the eggs, so that they would hatch out, she grumbled away to the thrush at the top of the apple tree.

'I wish my father would let me buy my own ribbons,' said Henrietta. 'He has no idea how to choose the right colour blue.'

She was so cross that she stopped and stamped her dainty little foot. As she did so, six of the speckled brown eggs fell out of the basket and smashed, squelch splodge, on to the dusty path.

'Oh, bother!' said Henrietta, 'Never mind. I still have – um er – eighteen eggs left.' (She was no good at sums, not like you are.) 'There will still be enough chicks for me to sell at the market so that I can buy a new yellow dress and a pink hat with white ribbons. Then I will look so beautiful that a handsome traveller riding past is bound to fall in love with me.' She stopped and swung her basket to and fro as she dreamed her little dream. And six more speckled brown eggs fell out of the basket and smashed, squelch splodge, on the dusty path.

'Oh, bother!' said Henrietta. 'Never mind, there are still – um er – twelve eggs left.' (She was no good at sums, not like you are.) 'That will still be enough chicks to sell at the market. And I can still buy that yellow dress, even if I can't afford the pink hat.'

She said to herself, 'Perhaps the handsome traveller will be a prince in disguise. He will put me on his white horse and carry me off to his castle. There we shall be married and one day I shall be Queen.'

She dreamed a little more. As she dreamed she swung her basket to and fro. And six more speckled brown eggs fell out of the basket and smashed, squelch, splodge, on to the dusty path.

'Oh, bother!' said Henrietta, 'now there are only – um er – six eggs left.' (She was no good at sums, not like you are.) 'It's no use hatching them out. I think I shall eat them for my dinner.'

And so she did, with a plateful of golden chips and some baked beans.

Of course, although she enjoyed her dinner very much, it was not quite the same thing as becoming Queen. All her fine plans had just been dreams and, as she told herself before she fell asleep that night – never count your chickens until they are hatched!

Songs

How do you feel today?	*Play School Song Book*
One potato, two potato	*Apusskidu* v
When we are happy, full of fun	*New Child Songs* 29

A thought to share

It is good to make plans, but don't make them too early.

Are you listening, God?

Father God, show us that we should not always expect things to work out the way we plan them.

Dear Father, please teach us to be brave when we are disappointed.

Dear God, please help us to understand that people sometimes make promises they cannot always keep.

28 Caring for others 1

Theme

The cruel treatment of children in the early 19th century

Aim

To introduce children to *The Water Babies* and the reason for its being written.

Starters

Do you have to go out to work?
    Did children of your age ever have to go to work?
    When?
    Would you like to have to work down a coal mine, in a factory or even up a dark, wide, high chimney with no light at all?
    (Can be developed in the classroom)

Narrative

The Water Babies

Can you imagine what it must be like to climb up *inside* a huge, dark chimney in a big house? Long ago – more than a hundred years ago – little 'Climbing Boys' had to do this to sweep down choking black soot. Cruel men called sweep-masters made them do this awful work,and beat them cruelly if they did not go fast enough.

Charles Kingsley, who was the vicar of a church in Hampshire, wrote a book called *The Water Babies*. It was his way of telling people about the cruel way in which little children from poor families were made to do such dreadful work for very little pay. The book is about a chimney-sweep called Tom, who is about seven years old. Here is a short piece from the book.

> 'Tom cried when he had to climb up the dark chimneys, rubbing his knees and elbows raw and when the soot got into his eyes, which it did every day of the week; and when his master beat him, which he did every day in the week; and when he had not enough to eat, which happened every day in the week likewise.'

Tom gets lost in the chimneys and comes down the chimney into in a little girl's beautiful bedroom. He sees himself in a mirror – '...And Tom, for the first time in his life, found out that he was dirty; and burst into tears with shame and anger.' Tom ran away and, after strange dreams, was taken by the fairies who changed him into a water-baby. It is quite a hard story to read and you may find some of it difficult to understand.

Perhaps your teacher could read more from the story and tell you how the little chimney-sweep met strange people like the Doasyoulikes and Mrs Bedonebyasyoudid and what happened to Tom.

Songs

Hands to work and feet to run	*Someone's Singing, Lord* 21
I whistle a happy tune	*Apusskidu* 3
Stand up, clap hands,	
shout thank you, Lord	*Someone's Singing, Lord* 14

A thought to share

Just imagine how we would have felt if we had been sent out to work as a chimney sweep.

Are you listening, God?

Dear Lord, thank you for those people who spend their lives working to help others.

Thank you, Father, for people like Charles Kingsley who worked hard to give little children a better life.

Dear God, show us how we can share the good things in life with those who have little or nothing.

29 Caring for others 2

Theme

Nursing and Florence Nightingale

Aim

Giving children a brief insight into the founder of modern nursing

Starters

Who has ever been in hospital?
   Can you say why you had to go in there?
   How old were you?
   Who looked after you while you were in hospital?
   In what way did the nurses look after you?
   What sort of work do they do?
   Is it a hard job?
   Would you like to be a nurse? Why?

Narrative

The Lady with the Lamp

'Now what's the matter with you, little lass?' said a soft voice. It was the middle of the night and it was very quiet in the children's ward of the Shaftesbury Hospital.

Tessa turned over in bed and whispered, 'Nuffin'. I want my Mum.' She sniffled and whimpered, 'I'm thirsty.'

Staff Nurse Barlow stroked her hair and said quietly, 'I'll get you a drink.' When Tessa had finished her drink the nurse tidied up her bed and made her comfortable.

'I hate it in here,' said Tessa, 'I want to go home.'

'Nobody likes being in hospital,' whispered the nurse, 'but hospitals are much nicer now than they used to be. Not much more than a hundred years ago, hospitals were dirty and unpleasant places. The nurses were stupid old women who were not very clean themselves. But one woman changed all that.'

'Who was that?' said Tessa, feeling a little happier now. Nurse Barlow spoke very quietly, so as not to disturb anybody.

'She was Florence Nightingale. She lived a long time ago, before my grandparents were born. Florence had rich parents and they were very upset when she said she wanted to be a nurse. Nice girls did not become nurses in those days.

But she did become one and she even ran a little hosipital herself. Then there was a war in which British soldiers were fighting far away in Russia. Florence managed to take 38 nurses to the hospital for the sick and wounded soldiers.

She found that the hospital was filthy and crowded and the soldiers were not being properly fed or looked after. After a while, she and her nurses were able to look after the soldiers and care for them. Florence often went round the wards, at night, carrying a lamp, to see if the poor men needed anything.

She became known as 'The Lady with the Lamp'. When the war was over Florence came home and started a hospital where women were trained to become proper nurses.

So you see, if it had not been for Florence Nightingale hospitals might not be the clean, safe and comfortable places that they are now. Even if you don't like being here.'

But Tessa was fast asleep.

Songs

Love somebody	*Tinderbox* 16
O Lord! Shout for joy!	*Someone's Singing, Lord* 4
Sing a song of people	*Tinderbox* 18

A thought to share

Let us think quietly about those people who spend their lives caring for others.

Are you listening, God?

Thank you, Father, for those men and women who have spent their lives helping others.

Dear God, bless those people who care for and look after children.

Father God, look after people who cannot look after themselves.

30 We're all the same, really

Theme

The common characteristics of all people

Aim

To illustrate the equality of all people on earth.

The management of the subject of racial relationships is already familiar to most teachers, and this assembly is only intended to suggest that we should maintain the healthy attitudes now prevalent in all schools. Because the subject is now so commonplace there should be no need to discuss it and it is probably better to read the story and leave it at that.

Story

The Parrot and the Beetles

Once, in a far-away jungle, there lived a little green parrot. She flew from tree to tree, looking for her dinner. After a while, she saw, three plump shiny beetles eating a glossy leaf. One was red, one was yellow and one was blue.

'Mm. Yum yum, I like the look of you, red beetle,' said the parrot. 'I think I shall eat you for my dinner.'

'Oh, I am *much* too beautiful to be your dinner!' squeaked the red beetle. 'Why, I am such a brilliant red colour that I am often mistaken for a scarlet berry. Besides, I am the colour of the setting sun as it goes to sleep after the heat of the day.'

'Hum,' said the parrot, 'it does seem a pity. Mm, yum yum, I like the look of you, yellow beetle. I think I shall eat you for my dinner.'

'Oh, I am *much* too beautiful to be your dinner,' chirped the yellow beetle. 'Why, I am such a mellow yellow colour that I am often mistaken for a yellow pear. Besides, I am the colour of the midday sun, as it shines hot and golden down upon the jungle.'

'Hum,' said the parrot, 'it does seem a pity. Mm, yum yum, I like the look of you, blue beetle. I think I shall eat *you* for my dinner.'

'Oh, *I* am much too beautiful to be your dinner,' twittered the blue beetle. 'Why, I am such a cool blue colour that I am often mistaken for a juicy plum. Besides, I am the colour of the bright sky through which the setting sun and the midday sun both ride until it is time for the silver moon to shine.'

'Hum. Is that so?' said the parrot. 'But then, even though one of you is red, one of you is yellow and one of you is blue, you are all equally tasty. It is what is under the skin that matters not what colour you are. Besides, it is my dinner-time and I am very hungry.'

So the green parrot ate them all. She ate the red one first, the yellow one next and the blue one last of all. And she enjoyed each one as much as the others.

Songs

I'd like to teach the world to sing	*Apusskidu* 2
Paintbox	*Harlequin* 32
Sing a rainbow	*Apusskidu* 5

A thought to share:

We should do our best to understand that people all over the world belong to one family.

Are you listening, God?

Father of all of us, please help us to care about children everywhere.

Dear God, show us how to love one another and how to be kind to everyone.

Father, we know we are all your children and you love each one as much as another.

31 Are people really different?

Theme

The common characteristics of all peoples

Aim

To encourage children to see that, although we may be different in many ways, we are all alike in that we are human beings.

Starters

How do children differ from one another (sex, size, race, origins, hair, eyes, etc)?

In what way are the grown-ups in the hall/room different from the children? (Discourage personal remarks)

In what way are the children alike? (e.g. they are all children/under eight (may vary)/British (may vary)/attend XYZ school etc – it's up to you just how long you let this go on and whether you develop it or not.)

Summing up

Whatever our differences we are all human beings.

Story

The Everything Animal

Long ago in a far-off place, there lived some happy creatures. One sunny day, Frog was out for a hop when he saw a most amazing sight. Before his eyes was the strangest creature he had ever seen.

Frog was so surprised that he hopped as far as the Big River.

When he got there Frog called, 'Fish, Fish! I have just seen the strangest creature. Why, it had webbed feet. Just like me.'

'O! Whatever next?' said Fish. And she swam off until she came to the grassy bank by the Big River.

There, Fish called, 'Rabbit, Rabbit! Frog has just seen the strangest creature. Why, it could swim. Just like me!'

'O! Whatever next?' said Rabbit. And he hopped off until he came to the hump on the grassy bank of the Big River.

There, Rabbit called, 'Turtle, Turtle! Frog has just seen the strangest creature. Why, it was covered in fur. Just like me!'

'O! Whatever next!' said Turtle, and she swam off under the water until she came to the bend in the Big River.

There, Turtle called, 'Duck, Duck! Frog has just seen the strangest creature. Why, it was laying an egg. Just like I do!'

'O! Whatever next?' said Duck and she swam up the river until she came to the dam across the Big River.

There, Duck called, 'Otter, Otter! Frog has just seen the strangest creature. Why, it had a beak for a nose. Just like me!'

'O Whatever next!' said Otter and he swam up the river until he came to a little waterfall. As Otter looked at it, the strange creature swam out of a hole in the river bank and grinned at Otter.

'Why, what a strange creature you are!' said Otter. 'You have webbed feet just like Frog. You can swim just like Fish. You have fur just like Rabbit. You lay eggs just like Turtle. You have a beak just like Duck. And you can swim, just like me. You are different from all of us. Yet bits of you are the same as each of us.'

The strange creature smiled and said, 'That is true. I am different. Yet some of me is the same. But look further still, Otter. I am an animal, too. Just like all of you.'

Otter scratched his head, 'Yes, I can see that,' he said, 'But what are you called?'

'Why,' said the different-yet-the-same creature, 'I am a Duck-Billed Platypus. And, one day, I will live in Australia and nowhere else in the whole wide world.'

Songs

Sing a song of people	*Tinderbox* 18
The animals went in two by two	*Apusskidu* 38
You'll sing a song and I'll sing a song	*Tinderbox* 30

A thought to share

Be grateful for the beasts that crawl,
And care for all the creatures small,
Enjoy the sounds of birds that sing,
The world is full of lovely things.

Are you listening, God?

Dear Father God, we are glad to be your children and members of your wonderful family.

Lord, we know we are all different but let us be glad of it.

Father, teach us to love the same good things.

32 Looking after pets

Theme

The care of pets.

Aim

Reminding children that it is their duty to look after their own pets.

The most difficult part of this assembly will be controlling the flood of anecdotes, advice etc. that will come from the children.

Starters

Who has a pet?
  To whom does it actually belong?
  Who looks after it?
  In what way?

Summing up

Lead from individual situations to emphasising that it is all very well having pets but they must be cared for – *always* and not when the owner feels like it. Suggest that if pets are not looked after properly, then someone could be guilty of – and do not hesitate to use the word – cruelty.

Story

Humphrey's Great Journey

'We'll never see Humphrey again,' howled Alice, 'my dear little doggie that I've loved for years and years.'

'What a fuss,' said Nicholas. 'Anyway, Humph is my dog, not yours. You used to say he was smelly. But I don't think we will ever see him again. How ever did he get left behind when we moved house?'

His father shook his head and said, 'I don't know. He just disappeared. I looked for him for an hour but there was no sign of him.'

Mr Powell thought for a moment, then said to Nicholas, 'Did you say that Humphrey was *your* dog?'

'Of course,' said Nicholas, a little surprised by his Dad's question.

'In that case, who fed him and trained him and took him for walks?' asked Dad.

'Well, you did, I suppose. I did... er... now and again.' said Nicholas, looking fidgety.

'Oh, yes,' said his father, 'About once a year. Now, I am willing to get you another dog to take Humphrey's place.'

The boy's eyes lit up. 'Cor, Dad, would you? Really?'

Mr Powell said, wagging his finger at Nicholas, 'Yes... but *you* will have to train the new dog and clean up afterwards if it makes a mess. *You* must feed it, once a day, and fill its dish with fresh water, every day.' Nicholas nodded like mad.

His father went on, '*You* must bath it, *you* must take it to the vet if that needs to be done. *You* must take it for walks. And, most of all, *you* must teach it to obey and how to walk with a lead. If you do all those things, then perhaps it will really be *your* dog.'

Nicholas thought hard for a minute. 'OK, Dad. That's a deal,' he said.

His dad did not rush out and buy a new dog and I am afraid that Nicholas forgot all about Humphrey. So it was a big surprise, three weeks later, to open the front door and see, sitting on the doorstep, a dirty, tired dog, with sad eyes. But only one dog could wag his tail like this one was doing. Yes, you've guessed – it was Humphrey.

Nicholas bent down to pat him. But Humphrey trotted past him and into the kitchen where Mr Powell was eating his breakfast. Humphrey sat on the floor, and put his paw on Mr Powell's lap, his tail wagging busily away. Now, I wonder why the dog did that?

Songs

Daddy wouldn't buy me a bow-wow	*Apusskidu* 43
Pete was a lonely mongrel dog	*The Jolly Herring* 13
Where, oh where has my little dog gone?	*Apusskidu* 42

A thought to share

Think – do we we love our pets as much as they love us?

Are you listening, God?

Father, bless all pets and help us to take care of them.

Help us, Father, to remember that pets are living things,

All things bright and beautiful,
All creatures great and small,
All things wise and wonderful,
The Lord God made them all.

Learning and Growing

33 Do you really know best?

Theme

Heeding advice

Aim

To suggest to children that other people may have advice or knowledge which can be of value.

Starters

Who listens to other people's advice?
  Do you always follow it?
  Or do you sometimes think you know better?

Summing up

Listening to other people's opinions may be tiresome but, very often, they may have something to say that is useful, or even more than useful.

Story

Mr Pickle's Trip to the Country

Mr Pickle thought he was a very important person and never listened to what other people had to say, least of all his wife and children.

One fine day, he said to his wife and children, Daisy, Pansy, Petunia, Primrose, Zinnia and Marmaduke, 'We shall drive into the country today.'

Nobody wanted to go. Mrs Pickle had a meeting to go to and all the children had things to do. Mr Pickle, said, however, that it would do them good and that was that.

After a little while Mr Pickle parked the car in a country lane and said, 'Let's walk across this meadow,' and off he went, the children following slowly behind. After walking a little way, Mr Pickle said, 'Let's eat our watercress sandwiches! Under this oak tree.' He did not listen when Mrs Pickle said they were lettuce sandwiches, nor when Daisy said it was a chestnut tree.

He did not listen when Pansy said that the grass was wet nor when Primrose said that they were sitting on an ants' nest.

Marmaduke told him that a big, snorting animal, with very large horns and a ring through its nose, was coming towards them.

Mr Pickle did not listen, nor when Zinnia said that it was a very unfriendly bull. He patted Zinnia on the head and said, 'Oh, it's only a cow! It is too pretty to be a bull. Father knows best.'

Then they all ran away as the bull charged! Back in the lane, Mr Pickle said, 'It must have been a bull after all. Never mind, anyone can make a mistake. Let's have our picnic in the woods instead.'

The children told him it was full of brambles, nettles and gnats. They told him there might be a wasps' nest in there, probably snakes, and it was very muddy.

Marmaduke said he could see a notice which said, 'Keep Out. These woods are private.'

But Mr Pickle said, 'Nonsense!' and set off into the woods, by himself. The family went and sat in the car. He soon came rushing out of the woods – he was scratched, stung and bitten, had just missed being bitten by a grass-snake, and a man with a red face was waving a stick at him and telling him to clear off because the woods were private and couldn't he read?

Mr Pickle always listened to his family after that. In fact, he started to listen to everybody who had something to say to him – even if it did not seem to be important at the time.

Songs

For the beauty of the earth	*New Child Songs* 89
When Father papered the parlour	*Apusskidu* 34
You'll sing a song	*Tinderbox* 30

A thought to share

May we be patient and listen to other people, because they often talk sense.

Are you listening, God?

Dear Lord, teach us how to listen to others as you listen to us.

Father of us all, bless us all today. May everything we do be loving and helpful.

Teach us Father God, to listen and to hear.

34 Saying sorry doesn't hurt

Theme

Apologising

Aim

Illustrating the importance of apologising when you know you are at fault – and meaning it.

Starters

How do people become upset by others?

What can be done to make it up to someone we have annoyed or upset?

Summing up

An apology must be genuine and is really a promise not to repeat the misdemeanour.

Story

Prince Proud and Prince Puffup

Long, long ago, Prince Proud and Prince Puffup were always arguing about who had the better flag.

Prince Proud said that his flag was smart because it was bright red with two golden lions on it.

Prince Puffup said that his flag was much smarter because it was sky-blue and had *three* silver lions on it. The silly princes argued about their flags all the time.

Early one morning Prince Proud's soldiers marched up and down, shouting, 'Puffup's flag is like a rag, looks more like a laundry bag!'

The Most Important Knight of Puffup's army was so annoyed that he told his soldiers to throw stones at Prince Proud's soldiers.

Then Prince Proud's three Very Important Knights rode out of their castle, shouting, 'Puffup is a silly ninny and his flag looks like a pinny!'

Prince Puffup's three Really Important Knights came out and, soon, both armies and both princes stood, shaking their swords and spears and shouting rude names at one another. Then the cooks and jesters and kitchen-maids all joined in. The noise was awful.

When the noise was bad enough to make you go deaf, along came the King's youngest page, Percival.

'Is there going to be a battle?' he said, looking interested.

'Push off,' said Prince Proud. 'Nothing to do with you.'

'Not for page boys, anyway,' said Prince Puffup.

'What's the battle about?' said Percival, and the princes told him.

'Are you really going to fight about flags?' said Percival, trying hard not to laugh. I think you both have great flags. They are just *different*, that's all. Now why don't you just say 'Sorry' to one another?'

Prince Proud and Prince Puffup grunted, together, 'Huh.'

Proud said, 'Him first.'

Puffup said, 'No, him.'

'Now come on,' said Percival. 'Just say "Sorry" *at the same time.* And shake hands as you say it. Ready? One. . .two. . .three. Go!'

'Sorry', said the Princes, at the same time, as they shook hands.

Percival told them that they had to mean what they said, because saying 'Sorry' was really promising not to do it again. Even if they did not like it, they knew that the page boy was right.

Songs

If you're happy	*Apusskidu* 1
Try again	*Tinderbox* 58
When we are happy full of fun	*New Child Songs* 29

A thought to share

It does not matter who is first to say they are sorry as long as someone says it.

Are you listening, God?

Father of us all, teach us to mean it when we say we are sorry.

Father God, help us to make friends again when we have quarrelled with someone.

Dear God, we shall have this day only once. Help us not to waste it.

35 So you think you can do it?

Theme

Boasting

Aim

Suggesting that boasting is a form of behaviour that can backfire and make one look silly.

Starters

What is boasting?
   Who knows someone who boasts? (No names)
   Why is boasting a fruitless form of behaviour?
   What often happens to people who boast?

Story

Who's Afraid of that Stupid Cat?

The mice at 15 Cheddar Road were talking about their new neighbour.

'That new cat is making life a misery,' said Maisie.

'No problem,' said Mungo. 'I'll soon fix that.'

'The rest of the mice looked at him in amazement. 'Is that so?' said Grandad Magnus. 'I think she's too clever for you. And she's fast. Nearly got me last week.'

Mungo laughed. 'You are a bit old, Grandad. Not young and smart like me.'

'Don't be cheeky,' said Grandad, 'I was young once.'

'What are you going to do, then, Mungo?' asked Merle.

Mungo puffed out his chest and strutted up and down the living-room. 'Why, I'm going to tell the stupid animal to leave us alone. I'm not afraid of a silly cat,' he boasted, shaking his fist in the air.

Grandad Mouse grinned and said, 'We shall see.'

'All right, then!' shouted Mungo, running out of the mouse-house, 'I'm going. Right now!'

He was back in the mouse-house in less than half a minute.

'That didn't take long,' said Grandad. 'Did you tell the cat off, then?'

Mungo said, wiping his whiskers, 'Well, er, not exactly. She seemed to be – er – out. Mind you, I did make some pretty frightening noises in case she was there.'

'Oh, yes?' said Grandad. 'Still, you can try later.'

'I will, too,' said Mungo, 'you'll see.' He sat down to have his tea.

He had nearly finished eating when Grandad said, 'I've just seen that little old cat going past our hole.' Mungo choked on his cake and Merle had to slap him on the back.

'I – er – um. Can't,' he said, 'It's Friday the 13th. I've just remembered. Too unlucky.' Next day, Mungo had a bad headache, the following day he felt sick.

The next day Grandad said to him, when no one else was about, 'I think you have been very sensible, Mungo. You were very foolish to boast that you were going to tell that cat off. You know very well that mice do not argue with cats. Now tell the family that you were just showing off.'

And that is what Mungo did. Everybody thought he was very sensible not to tackle the cat and very brave to tell the family that he had only been boasting.

Songs

Let's pretend   *Tinderbox* 25
Make a face   *Tinderbox* 3
Mysteries   *Tinderbox* 40

A thought to share

Let us remind ourselves that it is no good blowing a trumpet if we do not know how to play it.

Are you listening, God?

Dear Father God, help us not to be too proud and boastful.

Help us, Father, how to do what we say we are going to do.

Teach us, Father, to remember that we are small people in a big world.

36 Caring about others

Theme

Helping others

Aim

Pointing out that we should help other people less fortunate than we are.

Starters

Has anyone has ever been in hospital or ill at home for a long time? (There's always one)

Did it cause problems – eg plaster cast etc?

Did anyone help with alleviating the problem(s)?

Was the patient able, or willing, to do anything in return?

Describe a person who takes the trouble to do things for someone who is having a bad time.

Story

The Not-so-good Neighbours

Ruth and Joe Smith, who are twins aged nine, live next door to Mrs Price, who is quite old. One day their mother told them that the old lady was in hospital after being knocked down by a car, when she was crossing the road. It was not her fault, because the car driver had taken no notice of a red light at a crossing.

'She is quite ill,' said Mrs Smith. 'She has a broken leg, which is serious when you are as old as she is, and she has no family to take her a few presents.'

She asked the children if they would like to go with her to visit Mrs Price and take her some flowers and fruit. But they were quite rude about the idea.

'I can't go. There's a cup match on the tele,' said Joe.

'Oh, I have a ballet lesson at two o'clock and I shall be far too tired,' said Ruth.

Mrs Green was very annoyed with her children but it made no difference. They were not interested.

But the twins were about to get a lesson they did not expect. As they cycled through the woods, a huge branch fell off a tree, just as they rode underneath it.

The next thing Ruth and Joe knew was that they were in hospital having their broken legs set in plaster.

They had to stay indoors because it was raining. They got sick of reading, sick of TV, sick of videos (they only had two and Mum would not go to the video shop), sick of computer games (they only had three and Dad would not buy them any more).

It was holiday time. They could not go to school, so they got sick of each other. Then, one afternoon, who should come in, but – Mrs Price.

She was with Mrs Smith, who had a huge bundle of comics and a pile of cartoon videos in her arms.

'Look who's come to see you,' said Mum, with a big smile, 'Mrs

Price bought these at a boot sale ages ago and thought you might like them.'

Of course, Ruth and Joe could think of nothing else to say but 'Thank you.'

Mrs Price stayed for ages, telling them stories about her childhood which they found very interesting.

When she had gone, the twins told each other how selfish they had been. They made up their minds that, when they were well again, they would do as much as they could to help people who cannot always help themselves. Now, isn't that a good idea?

Songs

Love somebody	*Tinderbox* 16
Sing a song of people	*Tinderbox* 18
You'll sing a song	*Tinderbox* 30

A thought to share

Ask yourself if you know how to be a good neighbour.

Are you listening, God?

Dear Lord, help me to be kind and loving to others.

Father God, make us strong so that we can help others, even we find it hard to try.

Do all the good you can
In all the ways you can
In all the places you can
To all the people you can
As long as ever you can

37 Working together

Theme

Cooperation

Aim

To suggest that even small people can do great things if they all work together

Starters

Ask about pictures of the Pyramids in Egypt.

Ask about the real thing.

The buildings were made from huge blocks of stone and the Ancient Egyptians had no modern machinery to help them. So who did all the hard work?

Summing up

The Pyramids were built by the efforts of human beings, small in relation to the magnitude of the project, but working in concert. Develop at your discretion in the classroom.

Story

The Mighty Ants

Once there was an Elephant who boasted to all the other animals, 'I am the strongest animal in the whole world.'

Little Red Monkey said, 'I bet you aren't stronger than Water Buffalo.'

'Hah!' shouted Elephant, 'Bring Water Buffalo to me and we shall see.' Little Red Monkey scampered off and soon came back with Water Buffalo who stamped, snorted and charged. Elephant flicked out his trunk and tripped her up. Water Buffalo crashed into the dust and Elephant trod on her. Oof!

'You win!' bellowed Water Buffalo. 'You are stronger than I am.'

Little Red Monkey said, 'I bet Rhinoceros is stronger than you.'

'Hah!' shouted Elephant, 'Bring Rhinoceros to me and we shall see who is the stronger!' Little Red Monkey scampered off and came back with Rhinoceros who stamped, snorted and charged at Elephant. Elephant stepped to one side and Rhinoceros crashed into Old Gum Tree. Then Elephant trod on Rhinoceros. Oof!

'You win! You're stronger than I am!' roared Rhinoceros.

'Smarter, too!' shouted Elephant 'Now who's next?'

Then Hippopotamus tried stamping, snorting and charging but soon went back to rolling in the mud.

Crocodile went home crying, and Snake ended up in a knot. Hyena ran away yelping and Leopard ran around looking for the spots that Elephant had knocked off him. So that was that. Well, almost.

Little Red Monkey's sister said, 'I bet you can't push down that old, twisted tree over by Yellow Rock.'

'Hah!' shouted Elephant. 'Easy!' He pushed, shoved and heaved. But the old, twisted tree would not fall down.

'I can find somebody stronger than you,' said Little Red Monkey's sister. Off she scampered. Five minutes later, there was a strange noise, like soldiers marching.

Tramp, tramp, tramp, tramp! The earth shook and even Elephant was nervous. Then came a *Crunch crunch munch munch*. With a creak and a groan, the old, twisted tree crashed to the ground in a huge cloud of dust.

Tramp, tramp, tramp, tramp! and away marched an army of … soldier ants!

'There,' said Little Red Monkey's sister. 'They may be small but many little creatures, working together, can be stronger than one big creature.' And Elephant had to agree.

Songs

God made the world	*New Child Songs* 3
I love God's tiny creatures	*Someone's Singing, Lord* 42
The ants go marching one by one	*Okki-tokki-unga* 36

A thought to share

Even if we are small we should do our best to do big things.

Are you listening, God?

Father God, please help us to try hard and work together every day.

Little drops of water, little grains of sand
Make a mighty ocean and a pleasant land.
Little deeds of kindness, little words of love,
Make this earth an Eden, like the heaven above.

Isaac Watts

Thank you, Father of us all,
For all creatures great and small.

38 So you wish you were someone else?

Theme

Envy

Aim

Suggesting that, although you may be envious of another, that person may actually be envious of you.

Starters

Who would change places with a famous person eg royalty, Prime Minister, pop star etc?

What are the disadvantages of fame? (lack of privacy, responsibility, personal danger, etc)

Who would like to be famous? Why?

Story

Aren't You Lucky?

Polly, a King Charles spaniel, looked down her little snub nose at the ginger cat. The cat was sitting in a cardboard box on the floor.

'What a scruffy animal you are,' said Polly. 'What are you doing here? Your owner doesn't look as if he could afford to pay the vet.'

Chopper opened his eyes. 'My master only has his pension so he hasn't got much money. But it's all right for you. I expect you live in a big, warm house?' he asked.

'Oh, yes,' said the dog. 'Six bedrooms, three bathrooms, a swimming pool. What one might expect, really.'

'You are lucky,' said the cat. 'Still, my old master looks after me and I get plenty of cat food and milk. I sleep on the rug in the living-room. In the daytime, anyway.'

Polly sat up and said, 'Really? I'm not even allowed in the lounge. I have to sleep in a basket in the laundry-room. It gets awfully cold in there some nights.'

'I bet you get the best food specially cooked for you,' said Chopper.

A little tear trickled down Polly's doggy cheek. 'Oh, yes,' she said, sniffing sadly, 'and I get sick of it. I'd give anything for a dollop of meat out of a can sometimes.'

Chopper looked puzzled and said, 'Yes, but you get fussed over and dressed up with pretty bows and collars and things. It must be nice to be special like that.'

Polly snorted and said, 'Would you like to be bathed every single week? Then be marched up and down at rotten old dog shows? And fancy being allowed out at night – on your own.'

'Yes,' said Chopper. 'But I don't always *want* to go out on a snowy night. My master may be kind but he thinks that cats belong out of doors at night. Whether they want to or not. Out I go, woosh, rain or snow.'

Polly sighed, 'I wish they'd let me out on my own,' she sniffed. 'All I get is "walkies" every morning with old Parkin, the gardener. He hates dogs. It's "Come on, get a move on, leave that tree alone." Old misery.'

'Well, it looks like I wish I had some of your life and you had some of mine,' said Chopper. 'I don't think I envy you, really.'

Polly had no time to answer – she was whisked in to see the vet and Chopper did not even have time to say 'Goodbye'.

Songs

Can anyone tell me that?	*Tinderbox* 6
Think, think on these things	*Someone's Singing, Lord* 38
You'll sing a song and I'll sing a song	*Tinderbox* 30

A thought to share

There is probably always someone worse off than you are.

Are you listening, God?

Help us, Father, not to envy other people.

Dear God, do not let us forget that other people are not always happier than we are, although they might let us think so.

Father of us all, show us that we can be happy without having a lot of money.

39 Everyone is someone

Theme

Everyone has a part to play

Aim of assembly

To suggest to children that everyone, whoever or whatever they may be, can be as important as the next person.

Starters

Whose job in school is most important?
  Why that particular job?

Would the school be any good without teachers?

Could the school function without ...helpers, domestic staff....
administrative staff... the headteacher?

Would society function less well without... (bus drivers, policemen,
doctors etc)?

Story

How Tina Triangle played her Part

(It will help if you have a metal triangle and bar striker to show to any
children who have never seen one.)

Tina Triangle had lived on a shelf in a music shop for so long that even
Mr Treble, who owned the shop, had forgotten that she was there.

One day Tina was asleep and dreaming about a marching band. In
her dream the trumpets tootled, the drums rattled and the tuba went
Oompah Oompah! Then, in her dream, they all stopped playing and
Tina sang, very clearly, 'Ting Ting. Ting Ting.' How proud she was!

Suddenly Tina woke up. Whatever could she hear? Was it... no, it
couldn't be... but, yes, it was! Tina could hear... a band! She could
hear a real band marching along the High Street. The bandmaster
twirled his big silver stick and threw it into the air as he marched
proudly along.

Then, of all things, the band stopped right outside the shop. Tina
wondered what was going on. A moment later, the shop bell tinkled.

She heard someone come into the shop and say, 'Good morning, Mr
Treble. I wonder if you can help us?'

'What can I do for you, Bandmaster?' said Mr Treble. 'Well, the man
who plays the triangle in the band has lost our only triangle,' the
bandmaster told him.

'Is it important?' asked Mr Treble.

'Oh, yes, it was the only triangle we had,' said the bandmaster. 'We
can't play the Ring-a-ding March without a triangle at the Mayor's
parade tomorrow. It is his favourite march, you know.'

'Oh, dear,' said Mr Treble, 'I don't think I have a triangle left in the
shop at the moment.'

'Oh, what a nuisance,' said the bandmaster sadly. 'What shall we do?
The Mayor will be most upset.'

Tina became very excited. She shivered and shook so much that she
fell off her dusty shelf and on to the floor, with a loud ringing sound.

'Well, I never,' exclaimed Mr Treble, scratching his head. 'Wherever did that come from? I didn't know I had such a thing in the shop.'

The bandmaster picked up Tina, polished her on his sleeve and said, 'Mm, it is rather small. Still, it makes a pleasant sound. I am sure it will be loud enough for the march. Thank you, Mr Treble.' He marched out of the shop carrying Tina very proudly. And how proud the little instrument was.

Tina Triangle knew then that everyone, however small, has a part to play, even when they least expect it.

Songs

Let's beat a song of praise	*New Child Songs* 71
Love somebody	*Tinderbox* 16
The music man	*Okki-tokki-unga* 44

A thought to share

Think quietly – the world is big and we are small but we all have a part to play.

Are you listening, God?

Father God, we know that each of us matters to you.

Lord, show us how to play our part in making this world a happier place.

Dear God, help us to know when we are needed.

40 Tittle tattle

Theme

Gossip

Aim

Explaining that spreading rumours can often cause problems, especially when they are unfounded. Children do not always recognise that repeating 'stories' is actually gossip. The practice can however, be quite hurtful, even at a relatively tender age.

Starters

Ensure no names are used.

Who knows of cases of 'stories' being told about another person, true or not?

What is this telling of tales called?

What problems can it cause?

How can it be overcome?

Summing up

It is better not to repeat gossip, even if there is a foundation of truth.

Story

Freddie Finewhisker is Alive and Well

Freddie Finewhisker was on his way home from Farmer Growboot's big lettuce field, when he trod on a wasp.

'Buzz off,' buzzed the wasp, 'I don't like being flattened by stupid rabbits.' And just to show he meant what he said, he stung Freddie.

Freddie said 'Blow!' and 'Bother!' and hopped home on one leg. On the way, he met Clarissa Cottonend, who could see that Freddie had hurt himself.

But instead of asking Freddie what he had done she rushed indoors and said to her mother, 'Mummy, Freddie Finewhisker looks ever so ill. He was hopping on one leg and groaning with pain!'

Mrs Cottenend said, 'Oh, poor little chap. I wonder if he has been bitten by that wicked fox, Sam Scarletcoat.'

She rushed out into the garden and shouted over the wall, 'Mrs Twitchywhisker, isn't it dreadful about little Freddie Finewhisker? That awful Sam Scarletcoat has nearly killed him! His mother must be dreadfully upset!'

Mrs Twitchywhisker said, 'How awful. Something will have to be done about that fox!' She rushed off to Topears Street to see Freddie's Mum.

On the way, she saw old Mr Twiddlewhisker and said, 'Isn't it sad about poor little Freddie Finewhisker?'

'Why?' said the old rabbit, 'What's happened to him?'

Mrs Twitchywhisker told him about Freddie. The old rabbit is a bit deaf so he did not hear her properly. He trotted off to the 'Nibble Inn' and told the landlord, Peter Pumpwhisker, that three foxes had attacked poor little Freddie Wotsisname, and he was in hospital.

Mrs Curlywhisker was sitting in the corner and only heard a part of what old Twiddlewhisker said. Straight away she left her lettuce juice to tell Freddie's Mum how sorry she was.

On her way, she met Mrs Wigglewhisker and said, 'Have you heard the dreadful news about Annie Finewhisker's little lad? He was attacked by ten foxes and he is very, very ill and may even die!'

Just then, who should come limping past them but Freddie himself. He touched his cap to them and said, 'Good morning. What a lot of wasps there are about just now!'

And this tale only goes to show that it is wise to keep long tongues where they belong – inside your cheeks!

Songs

Both sides now	*Alleluya* 33
Can anyone tell me that?	*Tinderbox* 6
If you're happy and you know it	*Apusskidu* 1

A thought to share

Tell yourself that if you can say nothing pleasant, it is better to say nothing at all.

Are you listening, God?

Father God, help us to know what is true and what is not.

Father, teach us not to talk unkindly about other people.

Dear God, bless us all today
And may the things we do
Be both kind and gentle
May what we say be true.

41 Being grateful

Theme

Gratitude

Aim

To suggest that one should be grateful when another person does
something for you.

Starters

Who can say they do things for other people?
   What kind of things?
   Do you always expect to be thanked?
   Do other people do things for you? What kind of things?
   What does it mean to be grateful?
   Is saying 'Thank you' enough to show you are grateful for a
kindness?
   How can you show you are grateful in other ways?

Story

Lulu Lamb and a Wolf

Lulu Lamb lolloped along in the warm sunshine of a new April
morning. She danced her way over the dainty daisies smiling in the
green meadow, going nowhere in particular and worrying about
absolutely nothing at all.

Lulu gambolled on until she saw an open gate. Now Lulu had never gone farther than this gate in all her little life. Her mother, who was very wise, had told Lulu about important things like not talking to strangers and never taking presents from strangers, but she had never said anything about open gates.

So Lulu, being a little lamb who likes to learn about things, lolloped through the gate and on towards the trees she could see in the distance. When she reached the trees she was very excited, because she had never seen so many trees all in one place at one time. So she stopped to wonder a little why they all grew there.

As she wondered, she heard a gruff and growly voice, groaning, 'Help me, oh, please help me!' Lulu, being a little lamb who liked to learn about things, decided to find out more.

Lulu lolloped into the little wood and saw, lying on the ground, a huge, furry creature. Fat, shiny tears were rolling down its long furry snout and the creature was making the most pitiful sounds.

'Oh, help me, little snowy lamb,' whimpered the furry creature, 'I have been trapped here for three days.'

'But what kind of creature are you, Mr Furry Animal?' bleated Lulu. 'I have never seen a creature like you before.'

'Why, I am a kind and harmless old wolf,' sobbed the furry creature. 'And my fine bushy tail is caught in this terrible trap. Please get me out.'

'How do I do that?' bleated Lulu.

The wolf said, 'Put your dear little foot on that red pedal near my fine bushy tail and press hard.' Lulu did as the wolf asked and the terrible teeth of the trap opened up. The wolf got up and licked his sore tail.

The little lamb bleated, 'Aren't you going to say "Thank you" to me for setting you free?'

The wolf bared his terrible teeth and snarled, 'No, little lamb, I am not.'

'Oo, what an ungrateful wolf you are,' cried Lulu. The wolf grinned, showing his terrible teeth again.

'It is *you* who should be grateful, little lamb,' snarled the wolf.

'Oo, why is that?' bleated Lulu. 'It was I who set you free.'

'Yes,' snarled the wolf, 'but you should be grateful that I have not eaten you, because I am a wolf and you are a lamb!' And away he went, snarling as he ran.

Now who do *you* think should be the grateful one – the lamb – or the wolf?

Songs

Love somebody	*Tinderbox* 16
One man's hands	*Alleluya* 61
When I needed a neighbour	*Someone's Singing, Lord* 35

A thought to share

May we always be grateful when someone helps us.

Are you listening, God?

Little deeds of kindness,
Little words of love
Make this earth an Eden
Like the heaven above.

Father God, give us hands that help and hearts that love.

42 Mind your own business!

Theme

Nosiness

Aim

Making the point that there is a distinction between healthy curiosity and nosiness.

It has to be recognised that young children are inherently curious but they also have a penchant for being nosey to the point of embarrassment.

Starters

How many children have 'secrets'?

How many of them would resent someone else pestering them to reveal what their 'secret' may be?

Summing up

Everyone needs their own space, free from uninvited inquisitiveness.

There is, however, a time when keeping 'secrets' is not always the best course of action. To use a well-worn cliche - a problem shared is a problem halved.

Story

Crispin learns a Lesson

(Note: If you have a family by the name of Parker in the school, you must exercise your discretion as to whether you tell this story or not. It loses its punchline if you use another name.)

Once, long ago, in the county of Hereford, next door to Wales, there lived a family by the name of Parker. They had five sons and the youngest of them was Crispin.

Now Crispin was a good boy, but he was very fond of minding other people's business. If he saw a pot boiling, he wanted to know if it was rabbit stew and, if it was, who had caught the rabbit and where.

If even two people were talking about anything in the market square, then Crispin would be there, ears and mouth wide open, listening to every word that was being said. He took no notice when told to go away. All he did was to stand a little way off and listen even harder, saying 'Fancy that' and 'You don't say', now and again.

People began to tire of his questions and decided to do something about it. So one day Daniel Boyce, the baker, went to see old Maribelle, the wise woman who lived in an old cottage high up on the hill called Toptump.

The old woman listened to what Daniel had to say, thought a little while, and gave him a powder saying, 'This will cure Master Parker's curiosity, see if it doesn't!'

Daniel baked some special sugar buns and gave one to Crispin next day, as he passed by the shop. The boy was surprised but still wanted to know what was in the buns. The baker told him of all the things that he had used – except the powder.

Crispin scoffed the bun and walked down the street, smacking his lips. He stopped to ask the candlemaker where he bought his wax. He listened to Obadiah Wills as he tried to borrow some money from old Scottish Malcolm.

Myrtle Pugh chased him away as he listened to her telling Veronica Thomas about her corns.

Then he realised people were pointing at him and screaming with laughter.

He looked at his reflection in a shiny pan on Tinker Morgan's stall. His nose was as long as – an elephant's trunk!

He ran home to his Mammy who told him that this was his punishment for being such a nosey little boy and serve him right.

The nose shrank back to its proper size by Tuesday. You may be sure that Crispin had learned his lesson and he never poked his nose into any one's business after that.

But, I have to tell you that, for the rest of his life, wherever he went, he was known as... Nosey Parker!

Songs

Can you hear?	*Harlequin* 33
Talking	*Tinderbox* 52
Thank you for my friends	*Tinderbox* 31

A thought to share

May we learn that wanting to know is not the same as needing to know.

Are you listening, God?

Father God, help me to know the best way to use my eyes and ears.

Please, Father, show us how to be helpful children.

Show us, Lord, how to find out what we need to know without annoying other people.

43 Politeness costs nothing

Theme

The common courtesies

Aim

To encourage children to say 'Please' and 'Thank you' at the proper time.

Starters

What do you say when you are asked if you would like something?
What do you say when you get it?
If you give something to a person and they do not thank you for it, how do you feel?
How much does it cost to say 'Please' and 'Thank you'?

Poem

Hector and a Visit to London

It is a pity when one sees
A boy who never will say, 'Please'.
Now Hector never tried to say
His 'Please', and 'Thank you,' night or day.
He'd call his Mother, and demand
That she would come and hold his hand.
Or tell her that he'd like a drink,
He never even stopped to think.
No matter whether dark or light
Early morning, late at night,
He got his Mother out of bed.

He didn't care what Mother said,
His angry Dadda used to bawl,
Which worried Hector not at all.
One day, to London, Mother took
The boy, who with excitement shook.
They travelled there to see the Queen
And enjoy the splendid scene.
They travelled on the Underground,
To see the Palace cost one pound.
But Oh! A Guard's horse kicked his head
The worried Guardsman cried, 'He's dead!'
They laid poor Hector on the grass
Just as the Queen was walking past.
The Queen said, 'Is the boy alive?
Because I have my tea at five.
He'd better come for tea and buns
And meet the Prince, my eldest son.'
Now Hector, hearing what she said,
Decided that he wasn't dead.
At five o'clock he took his place,
Hands together, all said grace.
The Queen said, 'Will you have some tea?'
Young Hector said, 'That's fine for me.
I'll have a cup, your Majesty.'
The Prince of Wales said, 'Well, say 'Please'
And 'Thank you' when you get your tea,
You're not polite, young Hector lad,
Your manners are extremely bad.'
And Hector found in half an hour,
That he'd been locked up in the Tower.
The silly boy was terrified
That he would spend his life inside,
He thought, 'They might chop off my head!

And I would really be quite dead.'
But it was just a Royal trick
Which left poor Hector feeling sick.
They let him out in just a while
He ran, not stopping for a mile.
Now Hector always is polite,
With 'Please' and 'Thank you' day and night.
He learned his lesson very well,
He won't forget that prison cell!
Two little words that mean a lot
And they should never be forgot.

Songs

If you're happy	*Apusskidu* 1
Morning has broken	*Someone's Singing, Lord* 3
Think, think on these things	*Someone's Singing, Lord* 38

A thought to share

People like to hear us saying 'Please' and 'Thank you' especially when we mean what we say.

Are you listening, God?

Father, help us to be polite at all times.

May we do the things we should,
To be to others kind and good;
In all we do in work or play
To grow more loving every day.

Father God, teach us that thanking people shows that we care about them.

44 Softly, softly, catchee monkey

Theme

Persuasion

Aim

To suggest that arguments are often better settled by gentle means rather than violence.

Starters

Who has had a really bad argument with someone?
  What happened?
  Was there a fight?
  If so, did it solve the problem?
  Or was there a talk about the argument before the fighting started?
  Which is the better way? Why?
  How was the argument sorted out?

Story

The Clever Schoolteacher

Once, long ago, in Africa, there lived a Great Chief who was very important and ruled over many tribes. Now, the Great Chief had a very beautiful daughter and whoever married her would, one day, become Great Chief in her father's place.

Hundreds of young men, some warriors, some merchants and some just princes who did nothing at all except look pretty, all wanted to marry the Princess, whose name was Sweet Flower.

Did they want to marry her because they thought she was the most beautiful woman in all Africa? Or because the Great Chief was very rich? I do not know.

The Great Chief did not know whom to choose from all these men.

Some of the warriors said they would be the General of his Army and go out to conquer lands for his Empire. Some said that they would capture his enemies and bring them back as slaves in chains.

Most of the merchants offered him gifts such as golden crowns and bracelets, diamond rings and necklaces. Some said they would give him a hundred elephants or fifty buffalo or ten tame lions.

The princes offered nothing at all apart from themselves. As one of them said, they were so beautiful they did not need to offer gifts, even for a Great Chief's beautiful daughter.

So the Great Chief decided to hold a contest. There was to be a hunt for a rare woolly monkey that lived deep in the thickest jungle in his kingdom. Whoever caught it should marry his daughter; because no one had ever been able to catch the rare woolly monkey.

Everybody set off to capture the woolly monkey. The warriors rushed into the jungle shouting and beating their spears on their shields so as to frighten the woolly monkey.

But the clever animal was not afraid of noise and hid in his secret place, and none of the warriors saw so much as a shadow.

The merchants took bags of gold into the jungle and shook the bags so the gold jingled and jangled. But the woolly monkey knew nothing about money and hid away in his secret place, and none of the merchants saw so much as a shadow.

As for the princes, they decided it was too much trouble. So they all went home and had a long rest.

On the day after, a poor schoolteacher went into the jungle and tied a bunch of ripe bananas to a tree and he sat and sang a song, while he played his harp, about a clever woolly monkey.

And the woolly monkey came out and ate the bananas and fell asleep, listening to the song. All the schoolteacher had to do was to pop the monkey in a box and take it to the Great Chief.

When asked how he did it, the schoolteacher said, 'Softly, softly, catchee monkey.' And he married the Princess and they lived happily ever after.

Songs

Maja pade – let's all be happy	*Tinderbox* 57
Mysteries	*Tinderbox* 40
You and I	*Tinderbox* 55

A thought to share

Isn't it better to shake hands with someone instead of shaking your fist at them?

Are you listening, God?

Father, show us how to be gentle and kind.

Lord of us all, forgive us if we make other people unhappy because we are bad tempered.

God, our Father, help us to make friends with people if we have quarrelled with them.

45 Keeping your promises

Theme

Promises

Aim

Suggesting that one should always try to keep a promise.

Starters

(Ensure no names are used.)

Who has been let down by someone who has made a promise and then broken it?

　　Was it an important promise?

　　How hurtful was it?

　　Who has ever made promises and not kept them? Why?

(See also Assembly 58 (Good intentions) on page 133.)

Story

The Market Trader

Once there was a market trader whose name was Jake. People who bought his pans said that they never leaked, his soap lathered well and his fat candles burnt evenly without any smoke.

All seemed to be going well for Jake, and it seemed as if he would soon be able to buy a donkey to pull his little cart up the stony roads to market.

One market day, however, everything went wrong. A sudden thunderstorm began and a blinding flash of lightning struck Jake's stall, melting all his pots and pans and soap and candles.

There was nothing left, save a few pieces of burnt wood and some twisted metal. Poor Jake – how was he going to look after his wife and four children now?

Soon, however, all his customers and other market traders came round, patting him on the back and telling him they would all help him to get over this bad time.

One trader said he would collect money from all the traders to buy new stock, another said he would build a new stall free of charge, and another said he would give him the wood for nothing.

It seemed as everybody had promised to help Jake and he went home feeling a lot happier. Next market day he walked to the town.

But, when he went around the traders and his old customers, asking for what they had promised, they all made some excuse for not being able to keep their promises.

Jake stood by the fountain, not knowing what to do. Then, he saw that an old man was standing in front of him.

'I will help you,' said the old man, handing Jake a bag full of silver coins. The old man said, 'This is for you. But, a year from now, you must repay me and give me twenty silver coins besides.' Jake was delighted and promised to do as he was asked.

Jake bought a new stall and stock, made enough money to buy a donkey and, in a year, had more than enough left to repay the old man.

One fine June day, he saw the old man again. 'Have you kept your promise, Jake?' asked the old man.

Jake said, 'Indeed I have. Here is your money. And because you helped me when I needed it most, I have added fifty more silver coins.'

The old man took the bag and looked inside. Then he gave it back and said, smiling, 'It is yours to keep. And may good fortune go with you, Jake, son of Philip, who keeps his promise.'

Then he was gone and no one saw him go. When Jake looked into the bag, it was full of golden coins.

All because he had kept his promise – even to a stranger.

Songs

Each day different	*Harlequin* 43
One two three	*Tinderbox* 65
Maja pade – Let's all be happy	*Tinderbox* 57

A thought to share

If you mean it when you make a promise you are more likely to keep it.

Are you listening, God?

Father, help me to keep the promises that I make.

Dear Lord, make me strong to make only promises that I know I can keep.

Lord, teach me to not to be too disappointed if other people break their promises to me.

46 How important are you?

Theme

Self-importance

Aim

To suggest that the world does not revolve around an individual.

Starters

Suppose you were the only person in the world – who would be the most important person in the world?

Who is the most important person in the world *now*?

You may think you are but does everyone else think so?

Summing up

You may think you are important but the world can survive without you...

Story

Calvin the Stupendous

'Oh, I feel really ill,' groaned Calvin. His mother put her hand on his forehead.

'Yes, it is rather hot,' she said. 'You had better stay in bed today.'

'Oh, no!' wailed Calvin. 'We're playing Gilbert Court School today in the Cup Final. They'll never win without me. I'm the captain and the best player in the team. You'll have to ring the school and tell them to put the match off.'

His mother did no such thing. All she did was to phone to say that Calvin was not well.

Next morning, Mrs Newton heard a terrible noise coming from her son's bedroom.

'Mum, Mum!' he yelled, 'I've got big red spots all over me!' Calvin had chicken pox. To hear him howl and wail you would think nobody had ever had chicken pox before. As he was eating his breakfast, Calvin said that the school play would have to be put off because he had the most important part.

While he was eating his dinner, Calvin said his Cub Scout Six was sure to come last in the Sports next week because he was the fastest runner in the Six.

At teatime, he said his school chess team would lose their match against Oaktree School the week after, because he was easily the best chess player in the team.

'They haven't got a hope without me,' he groaned.

But the school football team won the Cup Final by three goals to one and the chess team won their match easily, and his Cub Scout Six came first in the Sports.

Calvin said, as his mother plastered pink stuff all over his spots to stop them itching, 'I reckon it was just luck. That's what it was.'

As his Dad said, trying not to laugh, 'Of course it was, Calvin. How could anyone ever manage without you?'

Songs

Can anyone tell me that?	*Tinderbox* 6
Thank you for my friends	*Tinderbox* 31
Turn, turn, turn	*Alleluya* 32

A thought to share

The only person who thinks you are the most important person in the world is – you.

Are you listening, God?

Father God, help me to understand that other people have feelings.

We know, Father, that you care about all of us.

Dear Lord, we know that, to you, no one is more important than another.

47 Don't keep it all to yourself!

Theme

Selfishness

Aim

To suggest that selfishness can sometimes rebound.

Starters

Would you share your last two sweets with someone?
    Would that someone have to be a friend or relative?

Summing up

Sharing limited resources with others is very difficult, especially for children, if there is no personal relationship. It is, however, worth bringing the merits of unselfish sharing before the children.
    See also Assembly 48 (It's better to share) on page 111.

Story

Nug and his Piece of Meat

Nal jumped away just in time as Nug swung his club at her viciously. 'You leave my meat alone,' he snarled. 'I trapped that bear and it's mine. Go away.'
Nal scowled. 'You'll never eat all that! Why are you being so greedy? You always used to share your food with the rest of us.' Nug growled, stuck a lump of meat on the end of a long, sharp bone and held it over the fire. Soon the delicious smell of roast bear filled the cave.
    Ogog, Nug's brother, shook snow off his furs as he came into the warm cave.
    'That smells good,' he said, 'a bit of leg for me, please, Nug.'
    He jumped back from the fire as Nug swung his club at him and snarled, 'Keep off. This is my meat, not yours!'
    Ogog snapped back, 'You have plenty to spare! That meat will go rotten before you can eat it all.'
    'I'll eat it all, little brother, don't you worry,' said Nug. Days went by. There was lots of meat left, but still Nug would not share his food with the rest of the tribe.
    Then, one morning, Lala woke up and sniffed. What a horrible smell! She woke Unga who screeched, holding her nose, 'I dow wod id is! Id's that beat of Nug's. It's god off.'
    'What?' said Lala. 'What are you talking about?'
    Unga screeched, 'Nug's meat has gone rotten, just as Ogog said it would!'
    Then Nug woke up and smelt the rotten meat. The tribe hooted

with laughter as he picked up the meat and rushed outside the cave. He threw it as far away into the snow as far as he could. As he went back in he could hear wolves fighting over it.

After that, nobody would share any food with him when they did find some. Not that there was much to be found. Selfish Nug had to make do with any scraps he could find and he was pleased when the thaw came, because nobody would speak to him. He moved out of the tribe's cave and went to live alone, in a cold, tiny cave in the next valley.

It was his own fault. If he had shared his food there would have been enough for everybody, none of it would have been wasted, and he would still be part of the family.

I am sorry to tell you that Nug never had a chance to go back to live with the tribe. Before the next snows had been on the ground for one moon a bear ate *him*, while he was out hunting.

Songs

Both sides now	*Alleluya* 33
Don't you push me down	*Tinderbox* 26
Maja pade – Let's all be happy	*Tinderbox* 57

A thought to share

Remember that you can share worries as well as sweets.

Are you listening, God?

Lord, teach us not to be selfish.

Thank you, Lord, for all your gifts. Show us how to share what we have with those who are in need.

Father, teach us to do all the good we can wherever we can and whenever we can.

48 It's better to share

Theme

Fair shares

Aim

Illustrating that sharing fairly is the most sensible way to behave.

Starters

What is sharing?

Does it just mean giving other people things you don't want, anyway?

Should you always keep the biggest share for yourself?

Should you only share *equally* with close friends/relatives but not others?

Story

One Way to Share a Bicycle

Amy and Thomas are good friends. But they nearly quarrelled once. It was about a smart mountain bike that they had won in a competition in the local newspaper. (You could name your own local newspaper).

The trouble was, that they had won the bike between them, because they had both answered the same number of questions correctly in the competition. One Saturday, they went to the shop to collect the bicycle.

The shopkeeper, Mr Todd, said 'Who's going to wheel it out of the shop?' Thomas had grabbed the bike and pushed it out of the shop, before Amy could say a word.

'I'm older than you so I'll have first ride,' said Thomas and he got on the bike. The next thing he knew, he was on the ground and Amy was pedalling towards the park. Amy had given him a sudden push which knocked him off the bike.

Thomas caught up with her at the bandstand. He grabbed hold of the handlebars and they struggled so hard that they both let go and the bike fell over. The children rolled over and over on the grass, struggling, kicking, biting and pulling hair.

They stopped when they heard someone talking to them.

It was a little old lady, dressed in green, carrying a large yellow umbrella and a big red bag. Thomas and Amy looked at her.

'I can sort this out,' said the little old lady.

'Go on, then, show us how to share one bike between two,' said Thomas. The little old lady tapped the bike with her yellow umbrella and... it fell to pieces!

She picked up the handlebars and gave them to Thomas. She gave the saddle to Amy, the chain to Thomas – you can guess the rest. Soon they had half a bike each.

'There,' said the little old lady. 'Now the bike is shared between you.' The children began to cry.

'Oh, please, mend our bike and we'll share it,' howled Thomas and Amy together.

'How?' said the little old lady.

'We'll take it in turns,' sobbed Thomas. The little old lady nodded and smiled and waved her umbrella. The bits of the bike jumped out of their arms and... whoosh! The mountain bike was leaning up against the bandstand, as good as new.

As for the little old lady – she had vanished. Amy and Thomas never did find out who she was. You can be sure, though, that they took care to share the mountain-bike after that.

They even took turns to clean it!

Songs

Both Sides Now	*Alleluya* 33
Can anyone tell me that?	*Tinderbox* 6
Why does it have to be me?	*Tinderbox* 53

A thought to share

Sharing means giving away something that you would really like to keep for yourself.

Are you listening, God?

Father God, please teach us how to share what we have, with others who may have less than we do.

Dear Lord, we try to be unselfish, but it's an awful struggle.

Dear God, teach us to share jobs that have to be done.

49 Does it belong to you?

Theme

Stealing by finding

Aim

To point out that if someone finds an article, it does not automatically become their property.

Starters

What would you do if you found – a ten pound note; an umbrella; what might be a diamond necklace; a puppy; a handbag?
  Would you say nothing and keep it?
  Would you tell someone and then keep it?
  Or what would you do?

Summing up

Responses will vary, according to the nature of the object. Suggest that there is a correct procedure which is handing the article into the police, more usually done by an adult.

Explain that if they do this and the object is unclaimed, the police will notify them and they will be entitled to keep the find. (Bear in mind that, if the righful owner can prove title, it can still be claimed by that person.) Or... there might even be a reward!

Story

Finder's Keepers

This is almost a fairy story and you can believe it or not, just as you choose. All I know is that it happened a long time ago and it was my Great Aunt Jemima who told it to me.

Mr and Mrs Precious had a very pretty young daughter whose name was Pearl and they were very proud of her. She had delightful manners and was most kind to all who knew her.

But, oh dearie me, despite all this, Pearl had a very unfortunate habit. If ever she found anything lying on the ground, she would pick it up and pop it in the pocket of her pretty pinny. It might be a shiny silver sixpence, a tasty treacle toffee wrapped in paper or a pretty handkerchief edged in lace. Swoop, scoop, snatch, into her pocket it went, in the twinkling of an eye.

Now, one fine day, Pearl and two of her friends were playing in the park. Suddenly, Pearl stopped skipping and swoop, scoop, snatch, she picked up something from the grass. She was not quick enough to pop it in her pocket before her friends could see it. Besides, the strange object that looked like a small jug with a lid on it, was too big to fit into her pocket.

Rosalind said, 'I think that looks like Aladdin's lamp!'

Rosemary cried, 'I think it might be made of gold! You must hand that in to Mr Policeman Nickem straight away.'

'Certainly not,' scoffed Pearl, 'I found it and I'm going to keep it.' As she said this, she rubbed it on her sleeve to make it shine more brightly. Then she threw it away in a hurry as a cloud of red smoke puffed out of the top of it.

The red smoke rolled and billowed and then got thinner. When it disappeared, in its place stood a humpty, nasty little creature, as red as the velvet on Pearl's new coat. It had a pair of stubby, stumpy horns, a long, curly tail and a very nasty look on its face.

The three little girls squealed and clung to one another in terror and shrieked, 'Oo, Mr Red Person, who are you, what are you, where have you come from?'

The little red creature said, 'Never mind all that. You have let me out of that silly lamp, Pearl Precious and now you must feed me for ever. And I'm an awfully hungry sort of fellow, I'm afraid and I take a lot of feeding.'

Perhaps it was just as well that it began to rain at that very moment. Down it came, wetting the pretty dresses of the three little girls. As for the strange little red creature – well, frizzle, hizzle, sizzle, hiss! he just disappeared. So did the lamp.

And that was the very last time that Pearl ever kept anything that she found lying on the ground. The next time she found a silver sixpence, she took it straight to Mr Policeman Nickem. He told her that this was the right thing to do. Because if you find something it does not mean that you should keep it – if you do you are really stealing. In fact, it is called 'stealing by finding'.

Songs

A better world	*Alleluya* 60
I jump out of bed in the morning	*Okki-tokki-unga* 47
You and I	*Tinderbox* 55

A thought to share

Remember, if you find something, someone else has lost it and may be looking for it.

Are you listening, God?

Dear Lord, may we understand that we should not keep whatever we find.

Father God, help us to know right from wrong.

Father of us all, keep us honest in all we do.

50 Winners and losers

Theme

Competition

Aim

To help children realise that, in competition, there can only be one winner, whether individual or group.

Not all schools hold competitive sports, but the concept of winners and losers applies throughout all human activity.

Where you do hold school sports, however informal, the younger children are often desperately disappointed when some get awards and others don't. Most schools have methods of overcoming the difficulty but there comes a time when they have to encounter and overcome the disappointment of coming second – or last.

Story

Only One can Win

Long ago, before the White Men came across the Endless Sea and stole America from the Red Men, there was a Mighty Chief whose name was Thunder Buffalo and he was Chief of the great tribe called the Dakotas.

Now Thunder Buffalo was an old man and he knew that he would soon be called by the Great Spirit to dwell in the Tepees of Chiefs in the Happy Hunting Grounds, far, far, beyond the skies.

And, because he knew that his days were short, he thought long and hard about which of his three sons should be Chief after him and wear the White Buffalo Robe and the head-dress of a thousand eagle feathers.

Thunder Buffalo was blessed with three fine sons, tall and strong; but they were triplets, all born within the hour and he did not know which one was the first-born.

Leaping Deer could wrestle a young buffalo to the ground.

Swift Spear could hunt the buffalo all day and never seem to be weary. Running Horse could stalk a buffalo and get within ten paces of it without its knowing he was so close.

So Thunder Buffalo could not decide who should be Chief. At last, he decided that the three young braves should take part in a race.

The winner should be the one who would be Chief in his place. They were to run as far as the foot of the Tall Black Hills and swim up the mighty Red River to the Rainbow Waterfall. There they would capture a young buffalo and ride it back to Cunning Snake, the Medicine Man, whose fire burned in the centre of the village.

The three brothers ran and swam and captured their buffaloes and took them to the Medicine Man who was waiting with all the Dakota people, too many to count.

The first to arrive was Running Horse, and he was hailed as the next Chief of the Dakotas. Brother Leaping Deer covered his head with wood ash and wailed on the Green Hill of Coyotes for two days. Brother Swift Spear hid in the Forest of Wolves for two days and howled at the moon for two nights.

But they came to see that they were brothers of the man who would be Chief, and they went to his tepee and said they would serve him all their days.

He said, most kindly, 'My brothers, I understand your disappointment, but someone must be first and someone must be last.'

And this is the truth, however it may hurt.

Songs

Hands to work and feet to run	*Someone's Singing, Lord* 21
The world is big, the world is small	*Tinderbox* 33
Why does it have to be me?	*Tinderbox* 53

A thought to share

May we remember that there is no shame in losing if we have done our best.

Are you listening, God?

Father, show us how to be brave when we are disappointed.

Dear Lord, help us to understand that, in a game or race, there have to be winners and losers.

Father God, teach us that taking part is just as important as winning.

51 Don't talk – do!

Theme

Actions speak louder than words.

Aim

Pointing out that a purposeful action is of far more use than a great deal of gratuitous advice, especially when urgent action may be needed.

Starters

What action should be taken if asked for urgent (or even non-urgent) help?

Would advice or practical assistance be of more use?

Summing up

If a 'Never Talk to Strangers' theme emerges, this is better followed up in an appropriate assembly or at classroom level, according to school policy. This is, however, not the aim of this assembly and it might be better if any discussion is led away from this aspect at this time. Important as 'Strangers' may be, the assembly could become a bit messy.

Story

Emily goes for a Swim

One day, Emily went out for a walk with her grandmother's old dog, Blodwen. She had walked a little way along the canal bank when she saw an old bridge that she had never noticed before.

'Come along, Blodwen, let's find out what's on the other side,' she said, but the dog didn't want to. It decided to sit down.

'Please yourself,' said Emily, and started to cross the bridge. She got halfway across when the wooden planks on the old bridge gave way and Emily fell into the filthy water with a big splash!

She managed to grab a piece of broken plank which helped her to float. Emily did not like the idea of swimming in the dirty water and began to paddle herself towards the canal bank, keeping her head well above water. As she did so, a woman came along the path.

'Can you help me to get out, please?' said Emily.

'Hum,' said the woman, 'I suppose so. But do you know you should not swim in that canal? Besides, it looks as if you are not a very good swimmer. Now, if you want to learn to swim properly, I know a very good teacher.'

Emily, was very cold and very wet by now. She opened her mouth to ask the silly woman to help her out of the canal instead of going on about swimming lessons. All she did was to swallow a mouthful of water, which tasted awful.

The woman went on, 'I shall give you the phone number of this person who gives excellent swimming lessons. And her lessons are quite cheap.' She began to rummage about in her huge handbag.

Emily shouted, 'For goodness' sake, help me to get out of here! This is not the time to tell me about swimming lessons!'

'Oh, you rude child,' said the woman, snapping her hand-bag shut. You don't deserve to be helped.'

To Emily's surprise, she walked off, leaving the poor girl in the smelly water.

Fortunately, clever Blodwen had bolted home and Grandma had come in her car, straight away, with her next-door neighbour. Mr James had brought a rope and, soon, Emily was in her grandmother's house, none the worse for her dip.

But she did say to her Gran, 'I do wish people would realise that it is more important for people to get on and *do* something, not just talk about it, when another person is in trouble.' And Grandma said she was quite right.

Songs

The angry song	*Tinderbox* 9
When I needed a neighbour	*Someone's Singing, Lord* 35
With a little help from my friends	*Alleluya* 38

A thought to share

Doing something to help is worth a hundred speeches about helping.

Are you listening, God?

Dear Father, help us to make the most of today and every day.

Help us to do the things we should,
To be to others kind and good;
In all we do at work or play
To grow more loving every day.

Father God, help us to know when it is the time to talk and when it is the time to do.

52 Blame Mr Nobody

Theme

Owning up

Aim

Suggesting to children that owning up to a misdemeanour is usually the wisest course of action.

Starters

Is it better to take the blame if something gets broken? What happens if the offence is denied and then the truth emerges?

What is likely to happen if the damage is accidental but the culprit owns up?

Story

Marcus and the Glue

'Ooer,' said Marcus, looking at the sticky mess on the floor. His teacher had asked him to fetch the glue from the store room. The jar had slipped from his fingers and smashed to pieces on the hard floor.

He could hear Mrs Larkin's voice from the classroom. 'Are you coming soon, Marcus? I'm waiting for that glue.'

'I'll get into trouble over this,' he said to himself. He wandered slowly back to the classroom.

'Well, where's the glue?' demanded Mrs Larkin. Marcus shuffled his feet and looked at the floor.

'It's – er – broken, Miss. All over the floor. It was like it when I got there,' he said. Mrs Larkin looked at him, very hard.

'Oh, oh,' thought Marcus, 'Now I'm for it.'

His teacher said, sharply, 'Are you quite sure you didn't drop the jar?'

Marcus said, not looking at her, 'Oh, no, Miss, not me, Miss. That's how I found it.'

'Really?' she said, crossly. 'Jars of glue don't just fall off shelves all by themselves. Do they, Marcus?'

'Must have been Mr Nobody, Miss,' said Marcus.

Mrs Larkin snorted, 'Oh, yes, we know all about him, don't we? A busy little man in this school. Now get back to your sums,' she said and went to get the glue herself.

But what Marcus did not know, was that Mrs Blewitt, the helper from Class Three, had seen him drop the glue. Mrs Larkin found her clearing up the mess. Of course, she was soon told what happened. You can imagine just how pleased the teacher was!

Marcus got a terrible telling-off. Not for dropping the glue. But for not owning up. He got told off in front of the class and he felt very ashamed.

What was more, Mrs Larkin told his Mum when she came into school that evening. He got told off by his mother and his father and his Auntie Peggy and his Auntie Flo and his Granny. He was not allowed to play on his bicycle for a week and he had his pocket money stopped.

When Mrs Larkin heard him moaning to his friend, Cornelius in the playground next day, she could not help saying, with a laugh, 'You shouldn't have blamed Mr Nobody, should you, Marcus? Then you wouldn't have got into so much trouble.'

Songs

Think, think on these things	*Someone's Singing, Lord* 38
Try again	*Tinderbox* 56
You and I	*Tinderbox* 55

A thought to share

When you are doing something you shouldn't are you sure nobody is watching?

Are you listening, God?

Help me, Lord, to own up if I have made a mistake.

Dear Father God, make us brave enough to take the blame when we have done wrong.

Dear God, we shall have this day only once. Help us not to waste it.

53 Are you sure you're bored?

Theme

Boredom

Aim

To suggest that we all have times when we are bored but that there is no reason to be bored very often.

Starters

What is 'boredom'?

Should you long for something really exciting to happen when you are bored?

Summing up

It is possible to relieve boredom by doing something more mundane than driving a racing-car, hang-gliding, skating etc.

Story

Dexter's Strange Adventure

Dexter yawned. 'I'm bored,' he said to the television set. 'I wish I had something exciting to do.'

'Is that so?' said the television set suddenly. Dexter fell off his chair.

'Yes, it's me,' said the television set. 'Come closer.' Dexter, very frightened, did as he was told.

'Shut your eyes and don't open them again until I say so,' said the TV. The next moment Dexter found he was standing in a very hot, smelly place.

Strange howls, screeches and rustling noises echoed from the weird trees and bushes that were all around him. Then he saw, high up through the leaves, a huge beast.

Dexter felt himself going cold with fright, although the place was so hot and steamy. The monster had its mouth open, showing enormous teeth that must have been a metre long.

Dexter knew that the creature was a fierce dinosaur – he remembered it from one of his books. It was an Allosaurus and it seemed to fancy Dexter for dinner.

The boy ran away, as fast as his legs would carry him. He did not see the sticky, black, smelly mud in front of him and he ran straight into it. Gasping for breath he managed to struggle through it – it was just like treacle.

He stopped to sit on a tree stump, flinging himself on to the soft ground as huge insects, with wings two metres wide, whizzed over his head.

Dexter had no idea what he would do next. Then, out of a green pool in front of him, rose another terrifying head. The teeth were not as big as the first dinosaur's, but there were more of them and they looked very sharp. Then Dexter recognised this monster. He had seen it in his dinosaur book a few weeks before – it was a Phobosuchus, the horror crocodile.

He ran as the head moved towards him. It was as long as a bus and just as nasty as the first creature he had seen. Dexter ran and ran, not knowing where he was going, or how to get out of this terrible place.

Then he fell, on to soft, thick grass and everything went black.

When he opened his eyes, he was lying on the green carpet of his living room. There was a commercial for dog food on TV, and he was still alone. It had all been a dream – but why were his feet wet? And why was he so hot?

Dexter decided that if what he had just done was exciting, then he would rather be bored. Or, better still, go and find something interesting to do, instead of watching TV all the time. Besides, he did not want any more strange adventures like that.

Songs

All alone in my quiet head	*Tinderbox* 17
Each day different	*Harlequin* 43
Mysteries	*Tinderbox* 40

A thought to share

Think quietly about those people who are unable to walk and run as we can, yet are never bored.

Are you listening, God?

Father God, help me to make the most of every day.

Dear God, we shall have this day only once. Help us not to waste it.

Father, teach us how to make the best use of our minds and bodies .

54 Remembering

Theme

Conscience

Aim

To encourage children to own up to misdemeanours, because they are not always easily forgotten.

Starters

Who has ever read or seen *Pinocchio*?

Who was Jiminy Cricket? What was his job?

Who knows of anyone (no names) who remembered something they had done wrong, for a long time after the event? (More likely to be elderly(?) relatives/acquaintances)

Can anyone explain 'conscience'?

Story

Charles and an Apple

This is a true story and Charles, who is a real person, still remembers what happened, although it was a long time ago. It happened when your grandparents would have been about the same age as you are now.

Charles lived next door to John and Hugh and they were very good friends. Charles liked playing with the two brothers, because they had all sorts of toys that he did not. They had a huge model railway with which Charles was sometimes allowed to play.

They often played, too, in the brothers' big garden in which there were apple trees and plum trees and raspberry bushes. If it was raining, the three children were allowed to play in a small tent that was put up on the lawn. In there, they played games like Ludo and Snakes and Ladders, and they spent many happy hours.

But one day something happened that Charles would remember all his life. It had been raining and they had been playing Tiddley Winks but the sun came out. John, who was the eldest, suggested that they had a game of cricket. So out they went.

As they were packing up their game and putting the bat and ball away in the tent, Charles saw a green apple on the groundsheet that was the floor of the tent.

He said nothing to the two other boys, but put it in his pocket. He told John that his shoelace had come undone and sat down until they had left the tent.

Then Charles bit into the apple. He wished that he hadn't. He had never tasted such a sour apple. He screwed up his face and poked the apple under the groundsheet. Then he went home for his tea. Next day, he called next door and asked if John and Hugh were coming out to play.

Mrs Lock said they were not allowed out to play for a whole week. Mr Lock had found an apple in the tent out of which someone had taken a bite. When he had asked who had done it, neither boy had owned up. Of course, they were not to blame, were they? It was Charles who had done it.

So they were in serious trouble. Not for biting into the apple and then hiding it, but for not owning up. Mr Lock, who was a very strict parent, had given both boys a beating with a leather strap – parents did things like that in those days.

Charles should have owned up, but he said nothing. John and Hugh knew, though, and they did not play with him for a long time. They forgot about it after a few months, but Charles didn't. He is still ashamed whenever he thinks about it – and he will never forget it.

Songs

All alone in my quiet head	*Tinderbox* 17
Try again	*Tinderbox* 56
With a little help from my friends	*Tinderbox* 38

A thought to share

May we never put blame on to someone else if it is our fault.

Are you listening, God?

Teach us, Father, to own up when we have done wrong.

Dear God, help us to be brave enough to admit when we have lied.

Father God, teach us not to tell lies.

55 I have all I need

Theme

Contentment

Aim

Explaining that some people are happy with what they have – even if they don't have very much.

Starters

Who would like to win a million pounds?
  What would you do with it?
  Would you be any happier than you are now?
  Does a person have to be rich to be happy?

Story

What is Happiness?

One day a rich man, whose name was Stan Grubber, was driving through the Thick Forest in the county of Chopshire when one of the tyres on his Rolls-Royce car had a puncture.

He was very annoyed because he had left his mobile phone at home. This meant that he had to get out and start walking. After trudging through the forest and getting very hot and bad-tempered, he came across a pretty cottage with a thatched roof, tucked away in the trees. Outside, sitting on a chair, was an old man with his eyes closed.

'Morning,' said the old man, without even opening his eyes. 'What can I do for you?'

Mr Grubber said, grumpily, 'I've had a puncture. Can I use your phone?'

'Sorry, Mister,' the old man told him. 'I haven't got a phone. You'll have to walk to Stumpton Post Office, if you want to make a phone call. It's only three miles,' and he shut his eyes again.

Mr Grubber's face went bright red. 'Walk? Walk?' he said loudly. 'Three miles? You must be mad. Haven't you got a car I can borrow?'

The old man opened the other eye.

'No,' he said. 'Too much hassle, what with punctures and things.' He grinned. 'Like you've got. Tell you what, though. My old dog, Jess, will take a note to the Post Office for you and they'll ring Coles, the garage in Crossbridge for you. Come inside and have a cool drink while you're waiting.'

Mr Grubber wrote a note which the old man stuck inside the dog's collar, and off she went.

'You haven't got much in here, have you?' said Grubber, looking round the cottage. 'Why, I have a house with ten bedrooms and a swimming pool.'

'Oh,' said the old man, as he poured out some lemonade. 'Why aren't at you home using them, then?'

'Oh, I don't have time to use any of it,' said Grubber, 'I'm much too busy making a lot of money.'

The old man said, 'Not much point in having them, is there? Now I have my cosy little cottage, my pension, free firewood for my fire and old Jess to keep me company. All I want, really.'

As Mr Grubber drove home, he thought, 'How happy that old man was. Perhaps he really is richer than I am, after all.'

What do you think?

Songs

O Lord! Shout for joy	*Someone's Singing, Lord* 4
Raindrops keep falling on my head	*Alleluya* 58
Stand up, clap hands,	
shout thank you, Lord!	*Someone's Singing, Lord* 14

A thought to share

Do you think that the best things of all are free?

Are you listening, God?

Dear Father God, teach us that we can't have all we want.

Lord, thank you for the simple things that cost nothing.

Dear God, help us to understand that we don't have to spend a lot of money to be happy.

56 Pick yourself up!

Theme

Facing up to defeat

Aim

Explaining that people don't win every competition that they enter.

Some children think that entry into a competition means automatic success and, of course, they are often disappointed. They should, however, be encouraged to try again.

Starters

Who goes in for competitions? What kinds?

Before you enter, do you believe you are going to win?

What if you don't? Are you very upset? Or do you try again?

See also Assembly 50 on page 116 (Winners and Losers)

Story

You Can't Win Them All

Giles was only eight but he had just beaten ten-year old Kulbir Bains to become school chess champion and he thought he was The Greatest!

The following week he went on holiday with his family to an hotel in Devon. On Sunday morning it was raining, so he wandered into the lounge.

There, with a chessboard in front of her, was a girl who looked about the same age as he was.

'Hallo,' she said, 'I'm Rosie. Do you play chess?'

'Do I play chess?' said Giles, with a big grin. 'I should say I do. But can you?'

'Yes, I'm not bad at it,' said Rosie.

Giles looked disgusted. 'Is that so? You are... not bad?' he said scornfully.

Rosie nodded and smiled. Giles shrugged his shoulders and thought that he might as well play her. Anything was better than looking out of the window at the rain.

'This won't take long,' he told himself. Rosie set out the pieces on the chessboard and they started to play. An hour later, Giles wished he was somewhere else. They had played fifteen games and Rosie beat him easily every time. It was dreadful. He had never been beaten like this before, and he seemed to do nothing right.

Before Rosie could set up another game, he threw the pieces on to the floor and ran out of the room.

At lunchtime his father found him lying on the bed, still unable to believe what had happened. 'Whatever is the matter, Giles?' he said. 'Aren't you feeling very well?'

Giles told him how he had been beaten at chess fifteen times. What was even worse was how quickly he had lost each game.

'Never mind,' said his father. 'You can't always win, you know.'

'Yes, but I'm champion of the school,' squeaked Giles, almost in tears.

'That may be so,' said his father, 'but there is a great big world outside your school. And you are bound to come across someone who is better than you are – somewhere. And you have.'

Giles had to admit that it was no good being disappointed. Sometimes you win, sometimes you lose. This time, it was his turn to be a loser.

When he found out that Rosie was chess champion of England for children under twelve, he didn't feel too bad about it.

Songs

Can anyone tell me that?	*Tinderbox* 6
For all the strength we have	*Someone's Singing, Lord* 16
Try again	*Tinderbox* 56

A thought to share

There is usually someone who can do things as well as, or better than, you can.

Are you listening, God?

Father, teach me to understand that I can't win all the time.

Dear God, help me not to give up if I think I am losing.

Father God, show me how to try my best at all times.

57 Who's afraid?

Theme

Fear

Aim

To try to reassure children that, very often, their fears are unfounded.

Starters

Tell the children what *you* are afraid of (be frank but don't overdo it...) – spiders, horror films, caves, heights etc.

What scares *you* (the children)?

If you're scared of something (like the dark) what do you do to overcome your fear? (Sing, whistle, cuddle something precious – children are not usually embarrassed when these are discussed, but some discretion may be required)

Summing up

Children's fears are very real to them and, although many fears are irrational and some are quite imaginary, we must never be dismissive. You will have to play your response by ear.

Probably best followed through in the classroom and, even then, a one-to-one basis may be best.

Story

The Timid Spider

Sabrina was a very happy little spider who lived in the corner of a cupboard. She was very good at spinning webs but did not use them to catch flies. You see, she did not know what a fly looked like because she had never seen one. Sabrina lived on scraps that people dropped in the kitchen.

Then, one day, she saw a very strange creature. It had black fur, six legs, wings, and thick hairs that grew out from its head and waved about. The creature was stuck fast in one of Sabrina's old webs and was buzzing loudly.

The fly stopped buzzing when Sabrina walked across to see what it was. But when she saw the fly the spider nearly fell off the web. If it hadn't been sticky, she would have. She was very careful not to get too close to this strange thing.

Sabrina spoke first. 'You won't hurt me, strange creature, will you? I'm only a harmless spider. Please stop making that awful noise because it frightens me. Besides, I have never seen anything quite as horrible as you are. What are you?'

The fly could not believe his ears and said, 'I am a fly. And you are the strangest spider I've ever come across.'

'Why?' said Sabrina. 'What's strange about me?'

'I'm supposed to be scared of *you*,' said the fly. 'You are not supposed to be scared of *me*.'

'Oh,' said Sabrina. 'Why is that?'

'I'm a fly and you're a spider,' the fly explained.

'So?' said Sabrina.

'So spiders eat flies,' said the fly. 'But because you are such a strange spider, I am not a bit afraid of you. Now help me to get out of this sticky web.'

Sabrina scratched her tummy and said, 'You know, fly, I must have been afraid of you because I've never seen a fly before. And there is nothing wrong with being a bit scared of something you have never seen before. But I shan't be afraid of flies, ever again.'

Then she ate him.

Songs

Being a spider	*Play School Song Book* 21
I whistle a happy tune	*Apusskidu* 3
In a cottage in a wood	*Okki-tokki-unga* 24

A thought to share

Did you know that the bravest people are those who face danger when they are afraid?

Are you listening, God?

Father God, teach us to trust in you when we are afraid.

Dear Father, help us to remember that you are always with us.

Thank you, Lord, for looking after us.

58 Meaning well

Theme

Good intentions

Aim

Much the same as Assembly 45 – keeping promises once they have been made.

Starters

You can use the same remarks as Assembly 45 which are:

Who has ever been let down by someone who has made a promise and then broken it? (No names)

Was it an important promise?

How hurtful was it?

Who has ever made promises and not kept them? Why?

or

Who has ever heard someone say 'I meant to do/go/tell etc. but I forgot/it got too late/had left it behind etc.?

Is this breaking a promise?

Is this is bad as making a promise with no intention of ever keeping it?

Are people who *mean* well as much of a menace as those who break solemn promises?

Story

Mr Meanswell Lets Everyone Down

Mr Meanswell is really a very kind man but he often used to promise that he would do something and then forget to do it.

It was not that he never meant to keep his promises – he just forgot he had ever made them.

One day, he said he would take old Mrs Notsowell to the doctor's in his car, at four o'clock. Four o'clock came and went. No Mr Meanswell. The old lady had to call a taxi and, because she had missed her appointment, she had to wait for an hour to see the doctor.

Next day, Mr Meanswell phoned Mrs Notsowell and told her that he started to clean his car and the time had got on and... but Mrs Notsowell did not want to hear any more and she slammed the phone down.

He promised to perform some magic tricks at little Billy Chatterwell's birthday party. Mr Meanswell was good at magic. But he failed to turn up at the party and Billy's Mum had to rush out and hire a video. The children were very naughty and threw jelly at the tele because they had been promised magic not Mickey Mouse...

Mr Meanswell said he had been looking forward to the party but he had been practising his best trick of pulling a rabbit out of a hat. The rabbit had escaped and by the time he had caught it, the party was over. He had *meant* to be there and he was very sorry. Not that it made any difference.

Mr Chatterwell refused to play golf with MrMeanswell after that and Mrs Chatterwell refused to speak to Mrs Meanswell for months.

Then, one day, he was cured! He entered a competition in a newspaper with a First Prize of a million pounds. Mr Meanswell intended to post the coupon but he forgot until it was time to walk the dog. When he got to the postbox, the mail had been collected. He actually posted it next morning doing, for once, what he had meant to do.

He could not believe it, a month later, when he saw in the paper that only one correct entry had been received but it was too late to be judged. And can you guess whose entry that was? Of course – Mr Meanswell's. If he had done what he intended to do he would have won a million pounds.

You can be sure that, after that, Mr Meanswell *always* did what he said he was going to do and he never let anyone down again.

Songs

Each day different	*Harlequin*	43
I jump out of bed in the morning	*Okki-tokki-unga*	47
Try again	*Tinderbox*	56

A thought to share

It is better not to make a promise at all than to make a promise and then break it.

Are you listening, God?

Father, teach us how to do our best to keep a promise once we have made it.

Dear Lord, if we mean well, then help us to do well.

God, our Father, teach me to be a person upon whom others can depend.

59 Eating more than is good for you

Theme

Over-indulgence

Aim

Warning, light-heartedly, about the possible consequences of over-indulgence.

You may encounter the problem of overweight children, although this should be an exception rather than the rule with this age-group. If, however, there are obese children in the group, or you know there is a family background related to obesity, you should use your discretion.

An alternative attack would be on the wrong type of food, eg high-fat/sugar/salt. You should, however, still tell the story and hope it hits the target.

Starters

Is over-eating bad for you? Why?
What about over-drinking (soft drinks)?
   If it is, why?
   What are the consequences of over-eating?
   What are the consequences of obesity?

Or

Do we eat too much of the wrong kind of food?

What is the wrong kind of food?

What can be the consequences of eating the wrong kind of food? (Avoid being *too* alarmist)

What can be the consequences of consuming too much sugar?

Story

Maxi's First Flight

'I am sure that egg is much bigger than the others,' said Mr Oozlum Bird, looking at the four eggs in the nest, 'and it is a different colour from the others. Wherever did it come from, I'd like to know.'

Mrs Oozlum Bird snapped, 'I don't know. Birds can't count. Anyway, it looks perfect to me. Now go away. I must start sitting on them.'

Mr Oozlum Bird flew off to collect juicy grubs for his wife's dinner. In two weeks' time, the eggs went *Creak! Crack! Pop!* and the chicks hatched out. Anyone could see that one of the four chicks was much bigger than the others.

Her parents called her Maxi, the others being called Mini, Midi and Semi. Maxi had an appetite as big as she was. Two minutes after Mr Oozlum Bird had staggered back to the nest with his beak full of juicy grubs, they had all gone. Not into the wide-open beaks of all the chicks. Oh, dear, no. Most of them went – *slurp! gobble! gobble!* – straight down Maxi's big beak.

The other three chicks managed to get a beakful now and again but Maxi seemed to eat all day. She would probably have eaten all night too if Mr Oozlum Bird had not been too tired to go grub-hunting in the dark.

Week after week, Maxi opened her big beak and nine out of every ten juicy grubs went *slurp! gobble! gobble!* straight down her throat.

One day, the greedy chick said in a sulky voice, 'This nest is getting far too small for all of us.' The other chicks said that *they* were not moving out. Father said that he was too busy collecting juicy grubs to build an extension to the nest.

Soon, it became so crowded in the nest that Maxi began to wriggle and squirm and push and shove. And, with a cheep and a chirp and a flurry of feathers, little Mini fell out of the nest.

But, instead of crashing to the ground, she fluttered down gently through the air and landed safely. What is more, an hour later, she was flying beautifully.

Semi and Midi thought this looked good, so they jumped out and, in an hour, they were flying as well as Mini.

Maxi said, 'Well, if they can fly, so can I.' She launched herself out of the nest. Wheeeee! Splat! Maxi was so heavy that she made a hole in the ground.

Her mother was most upset but her father said it was her own fault. If she had not been so greedy, she would have been able to fly, just like her sisters. As it was, she did fly – just like a brick. Straight down!

Songs

All things which live below the sky	*Someone's Singing, Lord* 41
Cuckoo! Cuckoo!	*Harlequin* 20
Think, think on these things	*Someone's Singing, Lord* 38

A thought to share

It is easier to get fatter than it is to get thinner.

Are you listening, God?

Thank you, Father, for food and drink.

Lord, teach us to be wise enough not to eat and drink more than we need.

Dear Lord, help us to share what we have with others.

60 It pays to be honest

Theme

Honesty

Aim

Emphasising that honesty is the best policy.

Starters

What would you do if someone picked up a ten pound note off the ground and said, 'Is this yours?'

Story

The Honest Hunter

Long ago, before the Northmen came to this land and drove out the gentle people who lived here, there lived a hunter whose name was Robbie, son of Geoffrey. He hunted deer and bear in the thick, dark forests that covered much of the land.

One day, he was crossing a deep, rushing river on a rope bridge. But halfway across, he dropped his quiver, full of his best arrows, into the angry water. Robbie was dismayed because it was his finest deerskin quiver. He had made the arrows himself and they were straight and fine. Tipped with sharp iron heads, they flew true through the air, never missing their mark.

The river was too deep and too fast even for Robbie to dive in. He leaned from the bridge, but could not see where the quiver and arrows had gone. Robbie was just about to go home when he heard a voice that boomed all around, from nowhere and from everywhere.

'Look into the water, son of Geoffrey,' echoed the voice. To Robbie's astonishment, a hand in a silver glove came out of the water holding a quiver of arrows, glittering and sparkling in the morning sunlight.

'Are these your quiver and arrows?' said the voice. Robbie shook his head.

'They are not mine,' he said. 'They are made of silver and they do not belong to me.' The voice laughed, making the trees shake. Then the hand disappeared below the water.

But, almost straight away, it appeared again, this time in a golden glove holding a quiver of arrows that gleamed and glowed in the morning sunlight.

'Are these your quiver and arrows?' said the voice. Robbie shook his head.

'They are not mine,' he said. 'They are made of gold and they do not belong to me.' The voice laughed again, making the trees shake, and the hand disappeared below the water.

As it did so, Robbie saw, standing against a tree, a man, the whole of him glowing as if he had fire all around him.

'An honest man,' boomed the voice. 'I, who have no name that you can say out loud, am well pleased. Look on the river bank from which you have just come.' Robbie saw, not believing his eyes, the silver and the golden quivers full of silver and golden arrows and, beside them, his own deerskin quiver and the wooden arrows.

'They are yours to keep, for your honesty, son of Geoffrey,' said the glowing stranger. Then he disappeared.

This is how Robbie became a rich man. But he never gave up his hunting, because he loved that more than anything.

Songs

Can anyone tell me that?	*Tinderbox* 6
Maja pade – Let's all be happy	*Tinderbox* 57
O Lord! Shout for joy!	*Someone's Singing, Lord* 4

A thought to share

People who are not honest are found out more often than they are not.

Are you listening, God?

Dear Lord, make our hearts loving.

Father, help us to be honest in all we do.

Father, may we learn from you how to be truthful children.

61 It's not a fib!

Theme

A lie is a lie whatever it is called.

Aim

To make children realise that words such as 'fib', 'whopper' and 'porkie' are only euphemisms for the word 'lie'.

Starters

What is a lie?

> Give some examples of words used for 'lie'.

Summing up

'Fib' or other words sound nicer than lie but any un-truth or falsehood is just that, and there is nothing nice about a lie. (The question of 'white lies' is too complicated at this level.)

> If someone asks you what a 'porkie' is, you might, at classroom level, look at rhyming slang, with, say, Y2. Some of the children may know more than you do...

Story

Jester Jumble and a Fib

'Jester Jumble!' said Shortcrust, the Pastry Cook in the kitchen of King Munch's castle. 'You've been at the jam tarts again.'

> 'Who, me?' squeaked Jumble. 'Of course I haven't. As if I would without asking, even if I didn't know you'd say "No" like you always do. And, anyway, I don't like jam tarts. Especially raspberry ones.'

> Mrs Noshup, the Chief Cook, said, 'And how, Master Jester, did you know they were raspberry tarts? Nobody saw them except Pastry Cook Shortcrust and me.'

> 'Oh ah well er um ee oo I... er. Perhaps I had er um ah um a little taste,' said the little jester, wriggling.

> 'You rascal, Jumble,' said Mrs Noshup, angrily. 'Not only have you

touched what does not belong to you. You have told me a lie about it, too. I'm ashamed of you.'

Jumble squeaked, 'Well, I only told you a little fib. A small whopper. A teeny porkie.'

'You've told a fib?' asked Wizzo, the Court Magician, who had just come into the kitchen for a cup of cocoa.

'Yes, he has,' Shortcrust told him. 'But what he really means is that he has not told the truth.'

The Court Magician looked angry and said, 'Do you mean to say, Jumble, that you told a... lie and called it a *fib*? This will never do. A fib, indeed.'

The Magician picked up his magic wand. 'I've a good mind to turn you into a sausage,' he said, sternly.

Jumble wailed, 'I don't want to be a sausage. I will never tell fibs again,' and hid under the table.

'*What* won't you tell again?' demanded the Magician.

Jumble said, trembling, 'I mean "lies", Sir, I won't tell "lies" again, Sir. Please don't turn me into a sausage.'

The Magician and the cooks burst out laughing, and Jumble knew that the Magician was too kind to turn anyone into a sausage. But Jumble always called a lie by its proper name after that, even if it sounded awful.

Because whatever you call an untruth it is still a lie.

Songs

Turn, turn, turn	*Alleluya* 32
Try again	*Tinderbox* 56
I whistle a happy tune	*Apusskidu* 3

A thought to share

May we be strong enough never to tell lies to get out of trouble.

Are you listening, God?

Dear God, show us that it is better to tell the truth.

Father God, teach us that the truth is stronger than lies.

Father God, please let our lips
Speak only what is true,
So all can trust the words we say
As we may trust in You.

62 What's luck got to do with it?

Theme

Nobody should rely on luck

Aim

To suggest that 'bad luck' should not be blamed whenever things go wrong.

Starters

Who knows a person who is lucky?

Why is that person lucky?

Are all successful people just lucky? Or is there something more to success than that?

Story

Who's a Lucky Piggie, Then?

One day, three little pink pigs heard that Waldo Wolf was coming to eat them. So each little pig decided to build a house to keep out the big bad wolf.

Pipkin made a little house of straw in only two hours and spent the rest of the day snoozing in a hammock.

Popkin collected twigs and branches and made a little house of wood in just one day and spent the rest of the week watching Porker TV.

But Pepkin built a house from bricks and mortar and took two whole weeks to finish it.

Then, one day, Waldo Wolf arrived. He had told his wife to heat the oven because he fancied some tasty roast pork and crackling, with apple sauce and sage and onion stuffing.

He knocked on Pipkin's front door and said, 'Are you thinking of having double glazing fitted? Let me in, and we can have a nice long talk about it.'

'Not likely,' said the pig, 'I know what you want. You're not coming in here.'

'Oh, yes, I am,' said Waldo and he huffed and he puffed at Pipkin's little straw house and blew it away. As he was getting his breath back, Pipkin ran to Popkin's little wooden house, rushed inside, slammed the door and hid under the bed.

Five minutes later, Waldo arrived and knocked on Popkin's front door. 'Are you thinking of buying the new wide screen TV? Let me in and we can have a nice long talk about it.'

'Not likely,' said Pipkin and Popkin. 'We know what you want. You're not coming in here.'

'Oh, yes, I am,' said Waldo and he huffed and he puffed at Popkin's little wooden house and blew it away. As he was getting his breath back, Pipkin and Popkin ran to Pepkin's little brick house, rushed inside, slammed the door and hid under the bed.

Five minutes later, Waldo arrived and said, not pretending to be a salesman any more, 'Look, you silly little pigs, I want my dinner and you are IT! Let me in or I'll blow this house down. Just like I did the other two.'

'You try,' said Pepkin. The wolf huffed and puffed and puffed and huffed. But he could not blow the house away. In the end Waldo had to go home and lie down for a week.

Pipkin said to Pepkin, 'My, you were lucky to have a strong little house like this.'

'Yes,' said Popkin, 'I wish we were as lucky as you are. What a lucky pig you are to live in a house that Waldo could not blow down.'

Pepkin went even pinker than usual and said, most annoyed, 'It was my hard work that built this house, not luck. If you had not been so lazy, you could have done the same. Just don't tell me how lucky I am.'

And that little pink pig was absolutely right.

Songs

I whistle a happy tune	*Apusskidu* 3
The angry song	*Tinderbox* 9
Work calypso	*Tinderbox* 23

A thought to share

Hard work often gets rid of hard luck.

Are you listening, God?

Father God, teach us not to mistake bad luck for bad work.

Lord, show us how to try really hard.

Father, bless our school. Teach us to work hard for you.

63 Keep trying

Theme

Patience

Aim

To encourage children to exercise a prudent amount of patience when tackling a task.

Starters

If you are doing some reading, do you skip the hard words?

Do you try to work out what the words are? Or do you guess what they are?

Or do you just tell yourself that you don't know them and carry on?

Will you ever learn to read properly if you keep on doing this?

What is patience?

Do you ever ask your teacher to help you?

Story

Why Giraffe has a Long Neck

Long, long ago, when there were not many animals in the world, Giraffe's neck was no longer than Camel's, although it was a little longer than Zebra's and much longer than Gorilla's.

For a long time, Giraffe could reach the leaves that grew on the lower branches of the trees and eat them easily.

Then, one dreadful day, a strange black cloud appeared in the forest. It whirred and rustled and no one knew what it was. Then the cloud settled on the lower branches of a Yum Yum tree, where the juiciest leaves grew.

There was a loud noise of munching and crunching. Then the black cloud moved on to the next tree, and the next, and the next. Soon, not one leaf was left on the bottom branches of a single tree.

Then the cloud left the forest, with a whirr and a rustle. The animals had a meeting, wondering what had happened.

'I know what that cloud was,' said Brown Bear. 'It was a swarm of insects called locusts. I do not know why they only ate the leaves on the bottom branches. They usually eat every leaf on every tree and leave them bare.'

Giraffe whispered, 'Whatever shall I do? I shall never be able to reach the tops of the trees. I shall starve to death.'

'I know,' said Lion. 'You will have to stretch your neck and reach as high as you can.'

So Giraffe stretched and stretched her neck while all the animals chanted, 'Try harder! Try harder!' But she still could not reach the top leaves.

'I can't do it!' she cried, but Lion told her to be patient and she would get there in the end. So Giraffe tried again as the animals cheered her on.

'I can't do it, I can't do it!' cried Giraffe as tears fell from her big eyes that had such long eyelashes.

'Yes you can,' said Lion. 'Keep trying and you will do it.' Giraffe had one more big try and then... 'I did it!' she shouted, and ate some leaves from the top branch to prove it.

'I told you so,' said Lion, 'Just by being patient.' Giraffe was very pleased with herself. But she had stretched her neck so much that she could not shorten it again.

And, ever since then, all giraffes have very long necks. I wonder if they are patient animals, too?

Songs

The animals went in two by two	*Apusskidu*	38
Try again	*Tinderbox*	56
With a little help from my friends	*Alleluya*	38

A thought to share

There is nothing to be ashamed of if we fail after we have tried our best.

Are you listening, God?

Father God, we shall have this day only once. Help us not to waste it.

Father God, make me strong to try again if I fail the first time.

Dear Lord, be with us whatever we do.

64 If at first you don't succeed

Theme

Sensible perseverance

Aim

Encouraging children who give up too easily when faced with a new situation. This theme is very similar to Assembly 63 on page 144 but looks at it from a different angle.

Starters

Who has tried to make something – a model or jigsaw – or has tried to solve a puzzle but has given up before finishing the job?

Why did you give up?

Could you not have had another try?

Summing up

More than one attempt to succeed can be worth the effort.

There also comes a time when a it is futile to continue with a task, especially if the wrong approach is being taken. (See Assembly 65 on page 149)

Story

The Caterpillar who Kept Trying

Caterpillar Number Forty looked around at her thirty nine brothers and sisters who were munching away at the green leaves.

Then she looked up at the sunshine that was peeping through the top of the tall tree where she lived.

'I wonder what's up there?' she asked.

Caterpillar Number Six stopped eating and said, 'Why? Caterpillars are supposed to eat, not ask questions. You won't find anything up there.'

But Forty had made up her mind. Off she scurried until her twenty little legs carried her on to the rough bark of the tree trunk. Then she saw Thrush, looking for breakfast.

'Oh, oh. I must hide,' she cried and hid in a hole until Thrush had gone. She set off again but had not climbed far when she saw Blackbird.

'Oh, oh,' she cried, 'I must hide,' and hid in a hole until Blackbird had gone. Then she saw Ladybird.

'Having trouble?' asked Ladybird.

'Yes,' said Forty, 'I'm on my way to the top of the tree and I've had to hide twice already. I think I'll give up and go home.'

'Oh, don't do that,' said Ladybird. 'You'll never reach the top if you let two birds put you off. Try again. You'll make it.' So Caterpillar Forty went on climbing.

Forty had to dodge Pigeon and Jay and then she saw Spider.

'Having trouble?' asked Spider.

'Yes,' replied Forty, 'I'm on my way to the top of the tree and I've had to stop four times already. I think I'll give up and go home.'

'Oh, don't do that,' said Spider. 'You'll never reach the top if you let four birds put you off. Try again. You'll make it.' So Forty went on climbing.

She had to dodge Greenfinch and Starling and then she saw Red

Ant. He told her just what Ladybird and Spider had told her – not to give up but to try again.

So Forty kept climbing until she reached the top of the tree. But, as she sat in the warm sunshine, she began to feel very odd.

She felt very fat and swollen, as if she was about to burst, and she felt very sleepy. Caterpillar Number Forty fell asleep on the leaf where she had come to a stop. She had turned into a fat, green chrysalis!

Forty slept for two whole weeks and, luckily for her, not a single bird spotted this juicy morsel stuck on a leaf at the top of the tree. Otherwise, she would have become a snack for some hungry bird.

Then, after a week in the sunshine, something began to happen to the chrysalis. POP! POP! POP! Its tough skin split and what should step out but... Forty! But she was no longer a fat, green caterpillar. Oh, dear, no – she was now a beautiful blue butterfly.

But the rest of her family, who had stayed at home, were gobbled up by Thrush, Blackbird, Pigeon, Jay, Greenfinch and Starling.

As for Caterpillar Forty, who was now a beautiful blue butterfly, she was sipping happily away at nectar in a honeysuckle flower and knew nothing about these dreadful happenings.

But wasn't it a good thing she did not give up when things were not going very well for her? Yes, she was a very lucky caterpillar indeed! Which is more than I can say for her thirty nine brothers and sisters.

Songs

Caterpillars only crawl	*Harlequin* 26
I watch the sunrise	*Alleluya* 15
Moving on song	*Alleluya* 39

A thought to share

May we have the strength to be patient and to try again, if things do not go right the first time.

Are you listening, God?

Dear Father, help us to try harder when we want to give up.

Please, God, make me strong so that I can finish what I started.

Father, make me wise enough to know when it is time to stop trying.

65 The time to give up

Theme

Judgement

Aim

Making children understand that there is a time when further effort on a task is fruitless.

Teachers will know children who often persist in struggling with a task, beyond the likelihood of success.

Starters

If you have a puzzle to solve and, after an hour, you could not do it, what would you do?

Summing up

Audience reactions are rather unpredictable in this situation so it will have to be played by ear. You should aim to arrive at the idea that there is a time to try hard but there is also a time to cry 'enough'.

Story

The Determined Otter

Octavius was a shiny little otter who lived near a deep, fast river. One day his Mother told him to take a fat trout to his Grandma who lived in the next holt, which is what otters' homes are called.

'But Mother,' said Octavius, 'the river is very high and running very fast between here and Grandma's holt, especially at the waterfall where there is a small whirlpool and it is dangerous just now. Do I have to go?'

'I know all that,' said his Mother. 'You will just have to try extra hard because Grandma has no food to eat. I can't go because I have to look after the twins. Your father has gone hunting again so I can't ask him.'

Octavius set off with the fat trout gripped firmly between his strong teeth. He dived into the racing water and began to swim up the river. It was hard work but he was a strong little otter and went a long way before he stopped for a rest.

All went well until he got as far as the waterfall. He could see that the water was racing fast and was very wild.

But the little otter swam as hard as his strong legs would carry him. He managed to reach the top of the waterfall, then suddenly he had no strength left. He was exhausted.

Before Octavius knew it, he found himself being swept away, back downstream. He rested for a little while and then set off again.

Once more, he reached the waterfall and almost fought his way to the top. But the current was too strong and he fell back to the bottom again, gasping for breath. Still Octavius would not give up. He struggled up the waterfall time and time again, but still he could not reach the top.

He floated, panting, in a quiet part of the river, with not an ounce of strength left in his little furry body. Then a familiar face appeared out of the water beside him. It was his uncle Sextus.

'You are having a hard time!' he said. 'Now, we all know that if at first you don't succeed, try, try, try again.' Octavius groaned.

Uncle Sextus said, smiling, 'But it is just as important to know when to stop trying. Sometimes, you can try too hard. Then you might just as well give up and think of a better way of doing things.'

'Oh,' said Octavius, 'What's that?' Uncle Sextus grinned an otter grin.

'Well, if it had been me,' he told him, getting ready to dive, 'I would have got out and walked *round* the waterfall. It would have been a lot easier than struggling to swim up it!'

Songs

Can anyone tell me that	*Alleluya* 32
Try again	*Tinderbox* 56
With a little help from my friends	*Allleluya* 38

A thought to share

May we always have the good sense to know when we have tried and lost.

Are you listening, God?

Thank you, God, for the chance to do good deeds.

Thank you, Lord, for the strength to do good deeds.

Dear Father God, help us to grow into caring people.

66 I've started so I'll finish

Theme

Completing tasks

Aim

To explain that one should always try to complete a job properly and with one's full attention.

This is quite a difficult concept for the younger children to grasp. The point to emphasise is that, if a finite job or project is started, then every attempt should be made to complete it, even if the activity takes some time. What should be stressed is that a new piece of work is not started until that current one has been completed, e.g. a piece of artwork. It may also be suggested that this attitude is just as important at home as it is at school.

Starters

If you have started painting a picture, should you start another one before you have finished the first? (It is a leading question...)

Story

Peregrine Bakes a Cake

Peregrine was hungry. The little pig looked in the biscuit tin. It was empty. He looked in the cake tin. Not even a crumb.

'I think I shall starve to death,' he groaned. 'I've eaten all the crisps. There's no bread to make toast. And the village shop is shut.' His tummy rumbled.

So Peregrine decided to bake a fruit cake. He found all the things that he would need – flour, sugar, butter, currants, raisins and an egg, the only one he had.

The little pig found a mixing bowl on top of a cupboard and a wooden spoon in the garden shed. He had to wash the bowl because it was dirty. He had to scrape and wash the spoon because he had used it to stir paint.

Peregrine lit the oven and, while it was heating, cleaned a baking tin which looked as if he had made gravy in it – a long time ago.

He greased the tin and then had to wash his trotters because he had greased them, too. At last, he was ready. He tipped everything into the mixing bowl, and broke the egg. Most of it went into the bowl but some of it slid down the table leg and on to the floor.

He stirred away at the mixture, very pleased with himself for having made such a good start. Peregrine popped the cake into the oven and sat down to watch 'Curly Tails' on Porker TV.

But, oh dear. Peregrine fell asleep. The next thing he knew was that someone in a blue uniform with shiny buttons was shaking him and saying, 'Come along, you silly little piggy, wake up. You nearly set your house on fire.'

Fireman Portly was shaking his shoulder and talking to him. 'I think your cake is cooked too much, Peregrine,' he said, holding out something black and smoking. It was Peregrine's cake! Mrs Bland, next door, had seen the smoke coming out of Peregrine's window and called the Fire Brigade. A little piggy tear trickled down Peregrine's pink snout and on to the fireman's big boot.

The fireman patted him on the shoulder and said, 'Never mind, you can always bake a cake another day. Just remember that a good finish is much better than a good start.

Songs

New things to do	*Tinderbox* 58
The super-supper march	*Apusskidu* 6
Try again	*Tinderbox* 56

A thought to share

We should always finish a job with the same excitement as we began it.

Are you listening, God?

Dear God, give us the patience to complete the jobs that we have started.

Thank you, Father, for all the interesting and new things that we learn each day.

Father, thank you for your patience with us.

67 Don't put it off until tomorrow

Theme

Procrastination

Aim

Pointing out the inadvisability of putting off until tomorrow what should be done today.

Starters

What does it mean when something is 'postponed'?

Is this the same as putting off something until another day because you can't be bothered to do it?

Why is it not a good idea to keep putting things off?

Story

Tomorrow may be Too Late

'Did you check my brakes, Norman?' asked Ted.

Norman the mechanic, who was working on the tanker lorry in the next bay, answered, 'No, I was going to do it tomorrow.'

'Well, do it now,' said Ted. Norman shook his head. 'Can't do that, mate. Can't leave this job to do that. It'll be all right. Tomorrow will do. You worry too much, Ted.'

Ted was still annoyed as he drove the huge tanker along the motorway. The night was very dark and the rain was lashing down. Ted whistled his favourite tune as he thought about his first stop.

'Just ready for a bacon sandwich and a cuppa at Daisy's Café,' he told himself. 'What a terrible night.'

But Ted never ate his bacon sandwich or drank the tea that he had thought about. As the rain eased off for a brief moment. Ted saw headlights coming straight at him. Someone was driving on the wrong side of the road!

He tried to turn his steering wheel to avoid whatever was coming at him and slammed on the brakes. The big tanker slowed as the brakes hissed, but nothing happened – the brakes were not working.

Ted did the only thing he could to avoid crashing into the other vehicle. He heaved at the steering wheel, the tanker skidded on the wet road, shot off the motorway and crashed down the steep bank. There was a terrible sound of crunching metal and breaking glass as the tanker turned upside down, its wheels spinning quietly.

Ted knew nothing about this – he had been knocked out when he hit his head on the driving-mirror. Luckily, there was hardly any other traffic on the motorway at the time. Ted was not badly hurt but he had to stay in hospital for a week.

The accident had been caused by an old man who had been driving the wrong way on the motorway. It was such a dark and rainy night that he had missed the right turning.

When Ted went back to work, he intended to give Norman a piece of his mind. But Norman was not there – he had been sacked when it was found that he had not done his job properly.

'Serve him right,' said Ted to the other drivers. 'It doesn't pay to put things off – they have to be done in the end. Never put off till tomorrow what should be done today. That's what I always say.'

Songs

Try again	*Tinderbox* 56
Wheels keep turning	*Apusskidu* 24
Work calypso	*Tinderbox* 23

A thought to share

Is it true that tomorrow never comes?

Are you listening, God?

Father God, help us to make the most of today.

Dear Lord. show us how to make the most of every day.

Dear God, we shall have this day only once. Help us not to waste it.

68 I'm no good at *anything*

Theme

Self-esteem

Aim

Persuading children that they can all do something well.

Starters

I am no good at... (whatever it may be, from crochet to oil-painting).

Are you surprised that I can't do xxxx? Can anyone do what I can't? (e.g. use video games, climb trees, etc.)?

None of you can do these things (fly a space-ship, speak Eskimo, or whatever), can you?

Can anyone do something that nobody else in the room can do?

(speak Gujerati, play the pipes etc.)

Ask for (a few) simple examples of what children can do (relate to the whole age-range of your audience) e.g. – X can use a word processor, Y can run faster than anyone else in the school, Z can swim 50m; these are all 'things they can do'.

Summing up

Everyone can do something. The fact that some do them better than others is irrelevant. (Those children who remain silent here may prefer to talk about themselves in the more intimate atmosphere of the classroom.)

Story

Miranda and the Plants

'Oh, blow the jigsaw,' grumbled Miranda. 'I can't get it to fit together. The bits must have been cut out wrong. Stupid thing.' She threw it on the floor in a fit of temper.

'I know,' she said, 'I'll watch that "Bambi" cartoon I had for Christmas.' She put the video into the player. Then she could not remember which buttons to press. After fiddling about for a few minutes, she screamed and began to stamp her feet. Her mother came in from the garden to find out what was the matter. But instead of telling her, Miranda sulked and said there was nothing wrong. So her mother gave up and went out into the garden again.

'I know,' said Miranda, clapping her hands, 'Mrs Poulter taught me how to knit in school last week. I'll finish that square I started.'

But that all went wrong – she had forgotten how to do the knitting and the stitches fell off the needles. Miranda decided to paint a picture but it went blotchy; she started to write a story but her pen went dry; she thought she would play her keyboard but she could only remember 'Greensleeves' and she didn't like that tune, anyway.

Miranda burst into tears and ran out into the garden. 'Mummy, Mummy, I can't do *anything*. I'm hopeless,' she sobbed. 'I'll never be clever like you.'

Her mother was kneeling on the grass and had been grumbling to herself. 'Is that so?' she said. 'Well, perhaps you can help me. I can't get hold of these tiny little plants to put them in the holes I've made. My fingers are too big to hold them without breaking them.'

Miranda stopped crying. 'I can do that!' she said. And, sure enough, because she had much smaller fingers than her mother, she could. She *could* do something that her mother could not do.

That made her feel a lot better. What is more, when she thought about it, she could do a lot of other things, too.

Songs

Hands to work and feet to run	*Someone's Singing, Lord* 21
If you're happy	*Apusskidu* 1
When we are happy, full of fun	*New Child Songs* 29

A thought to share

You will never know if you can or cannot do something if you don't try to do it.

Are you listening, God?

Dear God, show me how to make the best of myself.

Father, teach me about your wonderful world.

Lord, give me helping hands and a loving heart.

Special Days: Traditional Celebrations

69 Traditional New Year *January*

Starters

What year is it?
  What date is the first day of the year?
  What name is given to that day?
  What is a 'New Year resolution'?
  Tell us about some funny resolutions made at home at New Year.
  Have they been kept?
  Did you make any resolutions?
  Have you kept them?
  Why not (almost certainly…)?

Story

The New Year Bunolution

'I've had enough of that stupid fox,' announced Amos, gasping for breath. 'Nearly got me. It will have to go.'

Alfred, who was sitting in the corner of the warren, nodded. 'Quite right. You can't go anywhere in the fields now.'

Amelia stroked her fine whiskers and sniffed. 'Hah! That's all very well, Amos, *saying* that you are going to do something about that fox. But what are you going to *do*?'

Amos wiggled his tail and twitched his whiskers. 'Well, I heard humans at their New Year party last night when I was looking in the garden for some cabbages. They were making New Year resolutions. I thought I might do the same. About the fox,' he said.

'Oh, I heard that,' said Avril, 'One of them was going to give up smoking which I thought was very sensible.'

'There you are,' Amelia told Amos. 'Why don't you make a New Year resolution to tell that fox to clear off. You are more likely to keep a resolution if it's a New Year one.'

'What, now?' squeaked Amos.

'Oh, yes,' said Amelia, 'Make the resolution now. Then go out and tell that horrid fox to leave us alone. Straight away, before you change your mind. After all, if you make a New Year resolution, you should keep it.'

Amos gulped, but, brave little chap that he was, he marched straight out of the family warren and up to Silas Slink's den.

He was back home in less time than it takes to say 'Rabbit pie and chips.'

'That didn't take long,' said Amelia. 'Did you tell him?'

'Yes, I told him,' said Amos. 'But do you think it suits me not having a tail any more?'

Songs

With a little help from my friends	*Alleluya*	38
Why does it have to be me?	*Tinderbox*	53
Try again	*Tinderbox*	58

A thought to share

A New Year resolution is hard to keep because you are making a promise to yourself.

Are you listening, God?

Father of us all, thank you for the year that has gone.

Lord, help us to be brave in the year that is to come.

Dear God, please help us to keep our promises, whether to ourselves or someone else.

Poem

'First Foot', page 198

70 Shrove Tuesday – Pancake Day *February/March*

This assembly is designed to complement classroom teaching about the occasion.

A long time ago, Christians were expected to go without food, except very simple food such as bread, for forty days. This time was called 'Lent' and going without food, because you choose to do so, is called 'fasting'. On the day before Lent started people would eat up their tasty food in one meal – often in a big pancake with meat and other food in it. This is why we have a Pancake Day. Its proper name is Shrove Tuesday and the first day of Lent is called Ash Wednesday.

People in other faiths too have times when they fast. Nowadays, not many Christians fast, but a lot of people give up things they enjoy, such as sweets, for the forty days of Lent.

Starters

Who eats pancakes on Pancake Day?
  What is eaten with them – lemon juice, syrup, jam?
  Why are pancakes tossed?
  Who tosses them?

Story

Peregrine and Pancake Day

Peregrine is a little pig who is always hungry. One cold day, he looked at the calendar and said, 'Aha! Shrove Tuesday. That means... pancakes! Yummy. I just love pancakes.'

The recipe looked simple – flour, milk, eggs, sugar, a pinch of salt and some fat to cook the pancakes. Peregrine rubbed his trotters, said 'Easy peasy,' put on a pinny and started to collect what he needed.

He found his mixing bowl and started on the pancake mix which, so his book said, is called batter. He had his usual trouble with the egg, not all of which ended up in his mixing bowl, but the batter seemed all right after he had picked out the bits of eggshell.

Peregrine put fat in his frying pan and put it on the cooker to heat while he was beating his mixture. What the recipe did not say was how long pigs are supposed to beat the mixture before it becomes batter.

He thought he had mixed it enough when the smoke from his pan got so thick that he could not see the window in his little kitchen.

When the smoke had cleared, he washed the frying pan and heated more fat. Peregrine poured the batter into the pan. It sizzled and began to set. It was beginning to look like a pancake!

It wasn't exactly golden-brown – more of a blackish-brown, really, but, as he told himself, it was his first attempt. Even famous chefs had to start somewhere.

Then Peregrine remembered that the pancake had to be turned over. And, having watched the TV programme 'Perfect Cooking for Piggies', he knew just how to do it. He had to *toss the pancake!*

And so he did. The first time it stuck to the electric light bulb.

He scraped it off and tried again. This time it landed on the grandfather clock. He made another pancake and tossed that. It landed on the rubber plant.

He scraped that off, tossed it and it landed on the top of his TV. It was when the fifth pancake landed on the picture of his Great-Aunt Betsie that Peregrine thought there might be a better way to have pancakes for tea.

He went down to Mr Crumb, the baker, and bought a dozen pancakes. He sprinkled sugar and lemon juice on them and ate every single one. He felt sick after that, but, as he sat and watched 'Piggy School' on TV, he decided that it was worth it. After all, Pancake Day only comes once a year.

Songs

Mix a pancake	*Harlequin* 10
Shrove Tuesday	*Harlequin* 9
The super-supper march	*Apusskidu* 6

A thought to share

Isn't it wonderful that, if you toss a pancake, it usually comes down again?

Are you listening, God?

Lord, on Pancake Day, may we think of those children who have little or no food to eat.

Father, thank you for the fun of Pancake Day.

Dear God, thank you for all the good things that go into pancakes.

Poem

'Pancake Day!', page 198.

71 Mothers' Day

UK – March USA – May

Mothers' Day was, long ago, called Mothering Sunday. In March, on the fourth Sunday of Lent, the time when good Christians fasted, people were expected to visit the most important church in their part of the country. It would probably be in a town and was called the 'mother' church. Families met and talked when they made their visits and the day became a special day for mothers.

Mothering Sunday faded about seventy years ago. Then, during the Second World War, in 1941, thousands of American soldiers came to this country to fight the Germans. They told us about Mothers' Day in the USA.

Their Mothers' Day is in May and they give their mothers cards and gifts. A lot of British people seemed to like the idea and copied it. Many people now celebrate 'Mothers' Day'. A lot of children make a special effort to help their mothers on Mothers' Day.

Starters

Is Mothers' Day celebrated at home?
  Is Mother given cards – gifts – flowers?
  In what other ways is it made a special day?
  Who knows anything about Fathers' Day?

Story

Anna and the Flowers

Anna had been trying to save some money, but it was not easy. There was no money to spare at home. Her Dad had been out of work for a long time since the docks had closed down.

Anna wanted the money very badly because, on March 19th, it was Mothers' Day. Those of her friends who usually had money to spend were already chattering about what they would buy their Mums for Mothers' Day – chocolates, flowers, jewellery and lovely Mothers' Day cards. It all made Anna very unhappy and she wished she could do the same.

The only way Anna could get any money was to work for it. Old Mrs Turvey next door gave her a few pennies now and again if Anna went to the corner shop for her. Anna could not do Saturday work in a shop or do baby-sitting, because she was not old enough.

It was no use asking her Dad – he spent what money he did have on travelling around trying to find work. So what was she to do?

Anna walked to the shopping precinct on the day before Mothers' Day. She went with her friend, Kirsty, who had just fifty pence.

The girls spent a miserable hour staring at the shop windows, but there was nothing that Kirsty could buy for her mother for fifty pence, not even a tiny bunch of flowers.

'Let's look round the market,' said Anna. But the flowers were much too expensive even there.

The girls turned the corner into Old Moll's Lane. There, to their surprise, sitting on a stool, was a jolly old lady with rosy cheeks and a big smile. A big, striped umbrella was open behind her and, on the footpath,were buckets full of spring flowers of all kinds.

'Here you are, duck,' said the old lady, holding out bunches of pretty flowers. 'As many flowers as you like for ten bob.'

'What's ten bob?' Anna whispered to Kirsty,

'Ten shillings in old money. Fifty pence,' Kirsty told her.

Kirsty chose daffodils, the old lady wrapped them up and took her money with a beaming smile.

'Now what would you like, dear?' the old flower-seller asked Anna.

'I haven't got any money,' stammered Anna, trying not to cry.

'Oh, that doesn't matter, sweet'eart,' said the old lady. 'Your friend has given me enough for two. Just tell me what you'd like.' Anna chose the same as Kirsty and they dashed home to hide the flowers in Kirsty's garden shed.

Both Mums were delighted with their presents for Mothers' Day. Anna and Kirsty went back to Old Moll's Lane on the following Saturday, to thank the flower lady for being so kind.

There was no one there. Tom Trueman who kept the chip shop along the street said he hadn't seen any old woman at the end of the lane on the Saturday before. He said that the alley had been closed off by a gate for years.

He said that the girls must have imagined it all. But we know they hadn't, don't we?

Songs

How many people live in your house?	*Tinderbox* 19
Mama don't 'low	*Tinderbox* 21
Supermum	*Tinderbox* 24

A thought to share

Just think – one day you might have children of your own.

Are you listening, God?

Thank you, God, for the chance to thank our mothers on Mothers' Day.

Father God, let us be kind to our families every day.

Dear Lord, thank you for the love that our families give us.

Poem

'Mothers', page 199

72 Easter

This story is not intended to trivialise the real meaning of Easter. Young children tend to think more about Easter eggs and Easter bunnies at this time of year than about the most important festival in the Christian calendar. Teaching related to the fundamental aspects of Easter has to be related to the individual school status and philosophy and its obligations under the National Curriculum.

Those who prefer to celebrate Easter as a Christian festival may find *Assemblies for Primary Schools (Spring Term)*, by Margaret Cooling (See Bibliography on page 225) of value.

Starters

How is Easter celebrated at home?
  What have rabbits to do with Easter?

Story

The Easter Rabbit

Long ago in Wales, in a place called the Green Valley, there lived some very happy people. They were poor folk who made their living from keeping sheep on the slopes of the hills that looked down on the valley and they all cared for and did kindnesses for one another.

The grown-ups always celebrated Easter by giving little presents to the children. The girls were given tiny baskets, woven from reeds by the women of the village. These had pretty iced biscuits nestling inside them.

The boys were given stickjaw toffee, made by the men of the village. This was wrapped in mint leaves and put into little wooden boxes.

But one Easter not many lambs had been born and so there were few to sell at the market. This meant that there was no money to spare to buy sugar for biscuits and toffee. The men and women were very sad because they had given these little Easter presents to the children of the village for many years.

'What ever shall we do? What shall we give the children?' they asked one another when they met at the chapel on the Sunday before Easter, the day that is called Palm Sunday.

'Plenty of eggs there is,' said Jones the Milk.

'Fed up with eggs the children are,' answered Jones the Bellringer.

'I know what we can do,' said Mrs Evans the Goats, and soon all the village except the children knew all about her plan.

Early on Easter Day, all the women went into the woods called the Silent Woods carrying baskets. The baskets were covered with white cloths, but when the women returned home the baskets were full of wild flowers of all kinds.

After chapel on Easter Day, the children were sent to play in the woods. Some climbed trees while some picked primroses, and some looked for hazel nuts hidden by squirrels last autumn.

Then Blodwen Thomas cried out, 'I have found a strange blue egg!'

Thomas Rees called out that he had found a red egg! Will Harris shouted that he had found a green egg. Soon the woods echoed as the children found eggs of all colours – yellow, purple, orange, one even had black spots! Now the children knew very well what kind of eggs they were, but they were enjoying the joke.

'What kind of eggs can they be?' asked Gwyneth Williams.

'Too big for wild birds' eggs,' said Glenys Pugh.

'Same size as chickens' eggs they are,' called Dilys Morgan.

'There's silly,' said Glyn Jones, 'chickens don't lay coloured eggs like this!'

'I know what they are!' announced Billy Jenkins, who is none too bright.

'Oh,' asked Mary Lewis, giggling. 'What are they then, Billy?' Just then a rabbit ran out from under a bush.

'Well, they're rabbits' eggs!' said Billy, 'Anyone can see that!'

And, every Easter after that, the children went into the woods to look for rabbits' eggs. And, do you know, they always found them!

Songs

My Easter bonnet	*Harlequin* 16
Paint box	*Harlequin* 32
Rabbit ain't got	*Apusskidu* 37

A thought to share

An egg is a wonderful thing – how many sides does it have?

Are you listening, God?

Thank you, Father, for Easter time and the joy it brings.

Dear Lord, teach us to be grateful for the gifts we are given at Easter time.

Father, please keep us safe from harm in the Easter holiday.

Poem

'Easter', on page 200

73 St George's Day

St George's Day, which is on 23 April, may well fall during the Easter School Holiday, but you could tell this story, anyway, just for fun. Very little is known about St George, and children need only be told that he is the saint of England – the word 'patron' is best left until later.

Starters

What does the flag of St George look like?
    Where and when is it flown?
    The dragon is supposed to have lived in the county called Berkshire. Where is Berkshire?

Summing up

Any follow-up to the legend of Saint George and the dragon is best done in the classroom. Other patron saints are also best investigated there, too. So are 'dragons'!

Story

Saint George and Esmeralda

(This story has, if possible, even less foundation in fact than the original legend and is intended purely for amusement.)

An old story tells us that Saint George once killed a dragon that was making a nuisance of itself. The dragon was supposed to be a terrible monster, breathing out fire and eating people, as you or I would eat jacket potatoes.

Now I have to tell you that this was not the case. The truth is that there was, long, long ago, a little green dragon called Esmeralda. She was a little dragon who liked nothing better than to eat grass all day. Now and then, she might nibble a few buttercups, just by way of a change.

Esmeralda lived on a little hill which had a flat top, near the village of Uffington in the old county of Berkshire. She bothered no one and was most certainly not fierce. She would not even argue with a lamb.

The visit of Saint George to Uffington all came about because the Squire of the village did not like the idea of having a dragon living near the village. So he sent for the most famous dragon-killer in the land, Saint George. He is sometimes called King George, but I don't know why when he was only a knight.

Now, nobody knew it, but George had never killed a dragon in his life. Actually, he quite liked dragons and got rid of them by *singing* to them. His voice and the songs, which he wrote himself, were *awful*.

What is more, no dragon could stand the singing or the songs. Any dragon who heard Saint George singing one of his dreadful songs flew away as fast as its little wings would carry it.

Most of them went to live in Wales, where people are well-known for good singing and, for all I know, the dragons are still there.

So, one fine day in April, Saint George rode into Uffington to remove Esmeralda.

'You'll find this beastly dragon up on the hill,' said the Squire. Sure enough, Saint George found her grazing happily, on the pretty little hill with the flat top.

He shouted, 'I, Saint George, command you to leave, immediately!'

'Is that so?' said Esmeralda. 'And what makes you think I'm going to do that?'

'Oh, come on, be a decent little dragon,' said George.

'Make me,' said Esmeralda, going back to her dinner.

'Oh, well, you've asked for it,' sighed George, and he began to sing, in his awful voice, one of his awful songs:

'Ooooh! Dragon, leave this mountain,
Or I will dip you in the village fountain.
You most certainly cannot be allowed to stay
I must demand that you leave today.'

He stopped for breath. To his surprise, Esmeralda's colour changed from a lovely rich green, to a bright pink. All over, from the tips of her spiky ears to the end of her scaly tail.

'Oh, oh, oh,' whispered Esmeralda, 'that is the most bee-oot-i-ful song I have ever heard. It makes me want to cry.'

And she did begin to cry. She sobbed and sobbed, and fat green dragon tears ran down her scaly cheeks and on to the grass. Wherever the tears landed, the thick, green grass withered away and died.

Saint George, who could not bear to see a dragon crying, jumped on his horse and rode off as fast as he could.

Later Esmeralda had to move on to another hill to eat, because the grass on her little hill with the flat top never grew again. It never has, not even to this day.

The little hill with a flat top and no grass is still called Dragon Hill and you can find it on the way up the famous White Horse Hill in the county of Oxfordshire. But whether Esmeralda is still there, I really cannot say.

Songs

Let's pretend	*Tinderbox* 25
Puff the magic dragon	*Tinderbox* 50
The prehistoric animals brigade	*Okki-tokki-unga* 8

A thought to share

Aren't you glad there are no more dragons?

Are you listening, God?

Thank you, Father, for stories and poems.

Lord, may we grow to be strong like the saints of long ago.

Father God, make us brave to face the dragons of fear.

Poem

'A Dragon's Lament', page 200.

74 May Day

Pause for Thought

May Day is not a Christian festival and is almost certainly related to fertility rites of pre-Christian times.

May Day is a Public Holiday but this derives from the old 'Labour Day' and originates in the socialist political movement's tradition. It has nothing to do with ancient cultures.

May Day is still celebrated, however, in many parts of the country in the form of Maypole dancing which is still popular in not a few schools. Yours may well be one of them...

Starters

When is May Day?
Who knows anything that happens in some places on May Day? (e.g. The Hobby Horse custom in Padstow, Cornwall.)

Narrative

May Day was an important day in a lot of country villages but is not celebrated in the same way now in many places.

This reading comes from a book called *Lark Rise to Candleford* and tells us about the things that were done in some villages on May Day. This would have taken place when your grandparents were children.

At last came Spring which brought May Day, a most important day to the children of the village. The children did not dance round a maypole but they took part in a procession for the May garland, as it was called.

The May garland was made of big and small wooden hoops making a bell-shaped frame about a metre tall. On the last morning of April, children would bring to school all kinds of spring flowers, such as primroses, wallflowers and cowslips.

They used these, together with leaves, to cover the garland frame. At the top of the frame they fixed a bunch of the flowers called Crown Imperial. This bunch was known as the 'Top Knot'. A broomstick was pushed through the garland so that it could be carried.

On a little shelf at the front of the garland was placed a big china doll in a blue dress. The doll was known as 'The Lady' and the garland was carried in her honour.

The May procession would then set off. A boy with a flag and a girl with a money-box led the parade. Two older children, carrying the garland, came next.

Then came the May Queen, wearing a crown of daisies. Sometimes there was a May King, too. All the village children, aged between seven and eleven, followed.

Last of all came an older girl whom was known as 'Mother' and a boy called 'Ragman'. The grown-ups watched and cheered as they made their way to the vicar's house. There, they sang a song and some money would be put into the money-box.

The procession's next call was at the Big House where the Squire lived. He gave them five shillings, as it was in old money – twenty five pence, now. Then the children sang a song. One favourite was:

Come see our Garland green today,
First fruits of Spring, glory of May,
Cowslips, daisies, hyacinths blue,
Buttercups bright and primrose too.

After the Big House the children would visit all the farmhouses and cottages outside the village, often walking for miles.

Songs

A better world	*Alleluya* 60
I love the sun	*Someone's Singing, Lord* 12
Morning has broken	*Someone's Singing, Lord* 3

A thought to share

Always be as cheerful as the ribbons on a Maypole.

Are you listening, God?

Father, thank you for Springtime.

Lord, thank you for your lovely world.

Dear Father God, thank you for the chance to be happy

Poem

'The Maypole', page 201

75 Traditional Harvest Celebrations

Starters

What is a harvest?
   Is the farm harvest important?
   Is it as important now as it was many years ago? Why?

Story

Joe's Lucky Harvest

Joe Noakes did not know what to do. It was the end of September and it had been raining for three weeks.

The sun had come out on a few days, but only for a short while. His barley crop was beaten flat and was very wet, much too wet to be gathered by the big machines.

'I don't know what we are going to do,' he told his wife. 'I can't see us ever harvesting that crop of barley. We are going to be in trouble with the bank. If we can't harvest the barley we will have no money. And we owe money we borrowed from the bank to buy the new tractor.'

'What will you do with the wet barley if you can't cut it, Joe?' asked his wife, Ellie.

'I don't know,' said Joe, sadly, shaking his head. 'Just plough it in and get the soil ready for next year, I suppose. If there is a next year. If things don't get any better, we'll have to sell the farm.'

Joe waited until the sun came out and his fields dried up. On the first really fine day, out he went, to do what almost made him cry – plough in his lost crop of barley.

He had stopped to eat his sandwiches when he saw, through the window of the tractor cab, something shining in the wet soil. It was not very bright, but it shone enough to catch his eye.

Joe climbed out of his cab and went to take a closer look. At first he thought it was glass peeping through the soil. He bent down, still not sure what it was.

He got a garden fork out of his tractor and dug out the shiny object. The farmer wiped off the mud with his handkerchief, hoping his wife would not grumble too much when she saw it.

The thing looked like a collar, narrow on one side and wide on the other, very much like the sort of metal collars he had seen on pictures of some African women.

Joe rubbed at the metal with his sleeve and, to his surprise it shone brightly – just like gold! Perhaps it was...

The farmer took it to the local museum, who told him that it was a golden Roman necklace that had been buried in Joe's field for many years.

Not only that, but it was worth thousands of pounds. Joe Noakes was able to sell the necklace and his farm was saved by his lucky harvest. But I think Joe might have been just as happy with a good crop of barley.

Songs

Ears of corn are waving	*New Child Songs* 22
Look for signs that summer's done	*Someone's Singing, Lord* 54
The farmer comes to scatter the seed	*Someone's Singing, Lord* 56

A thought to share

The farmer has to sow the seeds long before he can gather the harvest.

Are you listening, God?

Father, we thank you for our food and for those who grow it.

Thank you, Lord, for those people who carry our food on ships, trains and lorries.

Father God, help us to remember those people who have little or no food to eat.

Dear God, we thank you for all your good gifts to us

Poem

'Cruel Winter', page 202

76 Hallowe'en and Trick or Treat

It is appreciated that Hallowe'en is not favoured as a topic in many schools nowadays, but children still celebrate it in their own way outside school. The increasing practice of 'Trick or Treat', imported from the USA, can upset some people; in any case it is not wise for children of this age to indulge the practice except under the right kind of supervision.

Neither the religious aspects of Hallowe'en, nor the links with witchcraft, are appropriate for this age-group.

Starters

Who knows about 'Trick or Treat'?
   In what country did it start?
   Has it gone on for very long in this country?
   Does anyone here play it?
   Whom do you call on?
   Who enjoys playing 'Trick or Treat'?
   Do the people upon whom 'Trick or Treat' is played enjoy it, too?
   Are you sure? Or don't you care?

Story

It wasn't Trick and it wasn't Treat

'Coming out tonight, Thomas?' asked Amy excitedly.

'Not likely. I bought a new computer game today,' said Thomas.

'You can't stay in tonight' said Amy. 'It's Hallowe'en! You know, Trick or Treat. When we knock on doors and get sweets and apples and things. None of the grown-ups mind. They know it's only a bit of fun.'

Thomas thought about it. Amy told him that there would be seven of them altogether, and he said he would come.

The children met by the village hall, wearing masks: two witches, three creatures from Outer Space and one gorilla. Little William Bone was wearing a Donald Duck mask.

Ryan Rumble laughed at William's mask so much that the little boy went home, bawling that he was going to tell his Mum and just wait till she saw Ryan's Mum.

The six who were left did not have much luck. They got two 'Clear offs'; one 'Push off before I set the dog on you'; one wrinkly orange; one toffee apple covered in fluff; three French francs; an old penny; and a pair of wet feet.

These belonged to Hayley Butler. Old General Smythe at Falklands Villa had told them to be off and stop annoying decent people or he'd call the police. Then he tipped a bucket of cold water out of an upstairs window. Most of the water landed on Kirsty, Hayley's sister and soaked her to the skin. She had run home, howling even more loudly than William had done. The rest of the water had landed on Hayley's feet, which is why they were wet.

None of the people they visited seemed interested in giving them a real Treat or letting them play a Trick, either.

Then Ryan had his bright idea. 'Let's go and call on old Mrs Page up at Mill Cottage. She's a silly old woman and she's bound to be good for a Treat.'

'You can't go there,' said Amy, horrified. 'She's about a hundred years old!'

'Oh, shut up,' snapped Ryan. 'We haven't done very well so far, have we?' Thomas was not happy about going up to Mill Cottage – he had been told off by Mrs. Page before. Ryan called him 'chicken' so he said he would go.

They trooped up the road to the Mill Cottage and rang the doorbell. The door opened. There stood old Mrs Page.

The five children shone their torches on to their masks. Mrs Page let out a terrible screech. The Trickers and Treaters were too scared to move.

But the next minute they were running down the road as Mrs Page came hurtling out of her door, carrying a withy broom (that is a broom made from willow twigs) screaming at the children and running nearly as fast as they were.

'You little devils! Frighten a poor, helpless old woman, would you! Come back here, you wicked children! You might have given me a heart attack with those nasty mask things. You come back here and I'll show you what I can do with a broomstick. I'll show you a treat and an even better trick!'

'Cor,' puffed Thomas, as they stopped for breath back at the village hall. 'Hundred years old is she? I'm jolly glad she didn't catch up with us, that's for sure.'

Gasping for breath, the rest of the children nodded and agreed. No more Trick or Treat for *them*. Maybe next year... ?

Songs

Halloween's coming	*Harlequin*	35
Hallowe'en is coming	*Tinderbox*	61
I whistle a happy tune	*Apusskidu*	3

A thought to share

Remember, what is fun to you may frighten other people.

Are you listening, God?

Dear Father God, help us to think about other people at all times.

Lord, please show us how to enjoy ourselves without scaring other people.

Dear God, we are glad that we have the chance to enjoy ourselves but let us not be selfish when we are having fun

Poem

'Trick or Treat?', page 202

77 Be safe on Bonfire Night   *November 5th*

At this time of year, most schools give their attention to the hazards of fireworks and bonfires. Many schools invite firefighters into school to talk about the risks and to reiterate the Fireworks Code, now well-established.

Starters

Who can tell us about the Fireworks Code?

Story

If Fireworks Could Talk

It was just getting dark on Saturday November 5th, and the Fireworks were lying in their tin box, talking.

'Are you looking forward to tonight, then?' asked Mega Rocket, looking down her blue nose and shaking her long tail.

'I should say so,' said Earthquake. 'I've been shut in a cardboard box on a shelf in a garden shed for over a week.'

'In a *cardboard* box?' asked Catherine Wheel. 'In a shed? Melvin's Dad smokes a pipe, doesn't he?'

'Were there any other fireworks in there with you?' asked Sparkling Diamonds.

'Oh, yes,' said Earthquake. 'There was Jumping Jack, Mighty Volcano, Silver Fountain and a lot of Fairy Sparklers.'

Fiery Rainbow said, 'Someone has been silly. Fancy putting a lot of us together in a cardboard box in a place where matches might be used. Anything might have gone wrong.'

'Never mind,' said Screeching Bomber. 'We're all right in this tin box, with the lid on. Melvin is not allowed to take us out or to light our blue paper. He is only six and isn't old enough to light fireworks yet.'

Diamond Rain told them, 'The boy was very silly last year, so I was told. He came to get my grandad out of the box and left the lid off. His dad did tell him off!'

Rainbow Waterfall nodded her blue paper. 'Oh, he did something much worse than that,' she said. 'His uncle had lit a Super Banger but it went out. And not only did Melvin go to have a look but he even picked it up! What a silly boy. It could have gone off in his face.'

'I'll tell you something else I heard,' said Roman Candle. 'He put one of my aunties *in his pocket!*'

Roman's brother went on, 'Yes, and he threw a Jetbomber into the bonfire! It was then that his Dad sent him indoors and he missed the rest of the show.'

'What a foolish boy he was,' remarked Space Ship, 'Still, he was only five. But he did do one thing right.'

'What was that?' asked Green Rain.

'He shut the cat under the stairs, before the party started,' said Space Ship.

'Look out!' cried Catherine Wheel, 'Here we go. Time for us to do our stuff.'

As she spoke, the lid of the tin was opened. The fireworks looked up at the stars and sang, altogether, very bravely, 'Here we go, here we go, here we go... ' But nobody paid any attention – the bonfire was crackling too loudly and the children were making too much noise.

Songs

Each day different	*Harlequin* 43
Tiger, Tiger	*Apusskidu* 41
When we are happy full of fun	*New Child Songs* 29

A thought to share

You may spend less than a minute being silly with a firework but more than a month in hospital afterwards.

Are you listening, God?

Father God, show us how to enjoy fireworks safely.

Dear Father of us all, help us to remember to look after our pets on Bonfire Night.

Dear God, teach us to think about other people on Bonfire Night.

Poem

'Fireworks', page 203

78 Hear the glad tidings!

Starters

Who ever goes out singing carols?
  Where?
  Should you always ask for money?
  What might be a good thing to do with any money that you are given?
  Who can name a carol?

Story

Mole, Rat and the Carol Singers

(This reading is an extract from *The Wind in the Willows* by Kenneth Grahame. The text has been paraphrased to fit most of the target audience.)

Mole had been staying with Water Rat in his home in the River Bank and wanted to see his own home again.

After some adventures, the two animals found Mole's home, lit a fire and soon made it warm and cosy. They found some food to eat and some beer to drink. As Ratty was preparing the meal, they heard shuffling feet and little, whispering voices in the yard outside.

Then they heard someone say, 'Clear your throats, then,' and 'Hold up the lantern, Tommy', 'No coughing after I count "Three"' and 'Where's young Bill, because we're all waiting.'

'What's up?' asked Ratty, as he opened a tin of sardines.

'It's the field mice,' said Mole. 'They go round singing carols at this time of year. Mole End is their last call and I always used to give them hot drinks and, sometimes, I'd give them supper.'

Ratty jumped up and opened the door. There stood ten small field mice, all wearing red scarves, their paws stuffed in their pockets and stamping their feet to keep warm. They giggled and sniggered and wiped their shiny little noses on their coat sleeves.

'One, two, three!' said the biggest mouse who was holding the lantern. Their breath puffed up into the cold night air as their shrill little voices sang merrily away.

'Villagers all, this frosty tide,
Let your doors swing open wide,
Though wind may follow and snow beside,
Yet draw us by your fire to bide;
Joy shall be yours in the morning.'

'Jolly well sung, lads,' said Ratty. 'Now come in and have a hot drink by the fire.' Mole was upset because there was nothing else for the singers but Ratty sent a mouse to buy food and drink at the nearest Mouse-shop.

Soon, they were all tucking into a hot supper and toasting their toes around the roaring fire. When they were full up and well-toasted, off they went, each with a little Christmas present for brothers and sisters at home.

Songs

Any songs from: *Carol, Gaily Carol*
Merrily to Bethlehem

A thought to share

If you are allowed to go carol singing, remember that not everyone is able to give you money.

Are you listening, God?

Thank you, God for carols to sing at Christmas time.

Lord, help us to remember carols are sung to remember the birthday of Jesus.

Father God, help us to think about those children who do not know it is Christmas.

We thank you, Lord, for everything that we enjoy at Christmas.

Poem

'Sing a Carol', page 203

79 Christmas trees

Starters

What kind of trees are Christmas trees?
  What do people often put at the top of their tree?
  What happens to Christmas trees after Christmas?

Story

The Proud Little Christmas Tree

Donna had kept on at her mother to buy the little Christmas tree. When her mother saw it outside the shop, she said it was no good because it was too small. But the little girl said it was the prettiest tree in the shop and it would look just right in their living-room. Her mother was tired after shopping and, when she saw that the tree cost two pounds less than any of the others, she gave in and said they would buy it.

Donna decorated the tree a whole week before Christmas. And what a proud Christmas tree it was. On the very top was a small, old fairy doll which had belonged to her Mum when she was a child. It was brought out from the box every year and given a new dress and wings.

Donna hooked on shiny coloured balls, red, blue and green; she clipped a tiny rocking horse onto one branch, a plastic robin with beady, black eyes onto another and finished it off with tinsel and plastic snow. On Christmas Eve, her Mum put on chocolates and a chocolate Father Christmas and then she fixed the coloured lights.

Everyone who came to visit said how pretty it all looked and the little tree seemed to glow with pride.

Christmas came and went and, then, a week after Christmas, Donna's mother said, 'This tree will have to go. The needles are dropping on to the carpet and they are driving me mad.' Donna sobbed and pleaded and begged her Mum not to throw the tree out.

In the end, Mum did not throw the tree out for the bin-men. Instead, she took it to the council yard. There, they had a machine which chopped up old trees into tiny pieces.

The man who was working the machine told Donna that this would be turned into plant food, called compost, and put on the flower beds in the park.

Donna did not believe him but, in the following spring, she saw hundreds and hundreds of dancing, yellow daffodils in the park. Then she remembered what the man had told her – her little Christmas tree had helped to grow these beautiful flowers for everyone to enjoy.

Songs

Any carols from: *Carol gaily Carol; Harlequin;*
                    Merrily to Bethlehem; New Child Songs etc.

A thought to share

When we decorate a Christmas tree, think of those children who will not know the joys that Christmas brings.

Are you listening, God?

Thank you, Father God, for all the joys of Christmas time.

Thank you, God, for the chance to celebrate the birthday of Jesus.

Thank you, Father for Christmas trees that cheer up our homes and remind us of the birthday of Jesus.

Poem

'Trees for Sale', page 204

Special Days originating in cultures not native to the United Kingdom

Only a brief background to each festival is given. Teaching about the principles of a particular faith, as required by the National Curriculum is, obviously, more appropriate in the classroom/group learning situation. So, too, are factual backgrounds as to the nature of the festival. Chinese New Year and Thanksgiving in the USA are examples of this.

This collection of stories is intended only as an assembly activity that can be conducted at or about the time of the festival in question so that any audience may participate.

Ideally, they should be told when the children have sufficient background knowledge of a particular faith or festival to appreciate a related story. The months quoted are those of the Christian calendar.

80 At the time of the Chinese New Year *Jan/Feb*

Pause for thought

Classroom teaching related to this event will not be a part of National Curriculum religious education. The festival is often introduced into schools because of its colourful and exciting atmosphere.

Narrative

The Chinese New Year is celebrated in many parts of the world where there are Chinese communities. It is a festival that lasts for two weeks during January or February.

Chinese people regard their New Year as Westerners do – a fresh start. They celebrate by offering gifts of wine and sweets to one of their gods, Tsao Chun, and enjoy a special meal of vegetables, fruit and cakes. Children are given red envelopes in which there are gifts of money. The celebrations feature the letting off of fire-crackers and dancing.

They also hang lanterns from trees and there is a Lion Dance. People, usually young men, move and jump and run under the lion's body, which is made of silk and paper. The lion has a wonderful painted head and its mouth, which opens and closes, is operated by the first man in the dragon. The lion dances through the streets, collecting money in red envelopes as it goes. These envelopes are hung from the shops that the lion passes as it dances.

Story

The Great Bell of Peking

This is a story from old China, although it is not a story about the Chinese New Year. It is supposed to have happened in the capital city of China, called Peking. This city is now known as Beijing and there are no more Emperors in China.

But, long ago, in the Year of the Monkey, a great Emperor ruled over all China. Yung-Lo, for that was his name, had decided that he wanted a great bell to go inside a new bell tower.

The task of making the bell was given to a man called Kuan-Yu, who was supposed to be the best maker of bells in China. First, he had to make, from finest clay, a mould which would be the shape of a bell. Into this, the bell-maker would pour a red-hot melted metal. This is called 'casting'. The metal Kuan-Yu used was bronze.

When the metal was cold and hard, it would be time to break the mould and, all being well, the bell would be ready.

After several weeks in making the huge mould, the Emperor and his court came to watch the melted metal being poured. But the mould cracked before the metal could set and the bell was spoilt.

The Emperor was very angry but Kuan-Yu was given another chance. This time, the mould did not crack, but the bell was full of tiny holes and was quite useless. The Emperor was furious and told Kuan-Yu that he had one more chance. If, however, the bell was no good this time, the bell-maker would have his head cut off.

Kuan-Yi was very frightened and told his beautiful daughter Ko-Ai what would happen to him if the third attempt failed. Ko-Ai loved her father very much, so she went to see a wise man who lived in the hills.

The wise man looked in his old books and said, 'The Great Bell can only be made if the blood of a good maiden is added to the molten metal in the mould.'

Although Ko-Ai was very upset at this, she told her father that, this time, the bell would be perfect.

The Emperor, his court and a huge crowd gathered for the third casting. Just as the stream of white-hot, molten metal rushed into the mould a huge shriek arose from the crowd. The brave young girl had jumped into the boiling, sizzling metal. Her father tried to grab her but all he managed to do was to hold on to her little shoe. He was led away by his friends, sobbing with grief.

After a while, the Emperor ordered that the mould should be removed. The bell was perfect and it was hung in the Bell Tower above the Royal Palace.

But the strange thing about it was that, each time it was struck a soft, low sigh was heard. *Hsieh! Hsieh!* This is the Chinese word for 'shoe'.

'Listen,' whispered someone, 'Poor Ko-Ai is calling for her shoe.'

And, from that day to this, when the Great Bell of Peking strikes, you can hear Ko-Ai calling for her shoe.

Songs

Can't help but wonder	*Alleluya*	34
Chinatown dragon	*Harlequin*	24
New things to do	*Tinderbox*	58

Thoughts to share

May we be able to understand the customs of people who are different from ourselves.

It is good to enjoy what is new and what is different.

Let us do all we can to learn from the festivals of people all over the world.

Poem

'Lion Dance', page 204

81 At the time of Hanukah   *December/January*

Background

Hanukah is the Jewish festival of light. It is the time when Jewish people celebrate their freedom. The festival lasts for eight days. During Hannukah, people exchange gifts and play games. It is, too, a special festival for children.

Passover, celebrated in March or April, is the most important feast of the Jewish year, but Hanukah has a less disturbing background than Passover so far as the younger children are concerned – Angels of Death and the demise of firstborn can be somewhat daunting for Infants.

Story

Not Enough Room

(This story has a meaning for followers of the Jewish faith, because, in many countries, Jews were not always treated very well and lived in bad, overcrowded housing. The story is based on one that probably originated in Eastern Europe many years ago.)

Jacob lived in a tiny cottage on the edge of a small village in the greenest part of Poland. Now Jacob and his family had plenty to eat. Their cow and goat gave them rich milk and tasty cheese and their six hens laid the fattest eggs you ever saw.

Jacob worried a good deal about his house. It was a smart house with white shutters and a roof which never let in the rain or snow. It had a good stone floor and a strong front door. But it was too small.

Jacob had a wife and ten children. So he went to see the Rabbi, whose name was Senesh.

'Rabbi, Rabbi,' said he. 'What can I do? My cottage has only one room and there are twelve of us living there.'

The priest scratched his head, thought and said, 'Don't you have a cow, Jacob?'

'Yes, I have a handsome cow,' said Jacob.

'Take the cow indoors with you,' said the Rabbi.

A week later the man went to Rabbi Senesh and said, 'Rabbi, the cow is so big that we cannot all sit round the table at the same time for our Sabbath meal.'

The Rabbi scratched his beard, thought and said, 'Don't you have a goat, Jacob?'

Jacob said, 'Yes, I have a splendid goat.'

'Take the goat indoors with you,' said the Rabbi.

A week later, the man went to Rabbi Senesh and said, 'Rabbi, Rabbi, the goat smells terrible and there is even less room in the house now.'

The Rabbi scratched his stomach, thought and said, 'Don't you have some laying chickens, Jacob?'

'Yes,' said the man, 'I have six fine chickens.'

'Then take them indoors with you,' said the Rabbi.

A week later, Jacob knocked at the Rabbi's door and said, 'Rabbi, Rabbi, we are all going mad what with the chickens flying about and clucking and the goat smelling and the cow taking up so much room. What can I do now?'

The Rabbi scratched his nose, thought and said, 'Put the cow, the goat and the chickens back outdoors.'

A week later, Rabbi Senesh saw Jacob and his family at the synagogue. 'How is it at home now, Jacob?' said the Rabbi.

Jacob beamed a big smile and said, 'It is wonderful, Rabbi. Since I put the cow, the goat and the chickens back outside, we have such a lot of room!'

Songs

A house is a house for me	*Tinderbox* 13
Hanukah	*Harlequin* 39
O Lord! Shout for joy	*Someone's Singing, Lord* 14

Thoughts to share

Let us be grateful for our own space at home or at school. Think kindly of those people who have no home of their own.

Let us be thankful that we have homes to live in, because many people do not.

Poem

'Rejoice for Light', page 205

82 At the time of Baisakhi *March/April*

Background

Baisakhi commemorates the day in 1699 when Guru Gobind Singh carried out the first baptisms into the brotherhood of Sikhs called the *Khalsa,* which means 'the pure ones'. ('Brotherhood' is not exclusively for men.) The festival is known as a *Mela*.

Story

The Poor Man and the Rich Man

(This story has no origins in Sikh folklore but is based on the Sikh belief in the equality of all people.)

There was once a good man who had worked hard and troubled no one for many years of his life. He had a fine family and a comfortable home. But, one terrible day, disaster struck his home village. A fearful earthquake destroyed the village and he was the only person left alive in a pile of rubble. Even worse, he himself was crippled by his house falling upon him and he became unable to walk.

The only way he could get about was on a little trolley and the only way he could buy a little food and drink was to sit in the main street of the city and ask for money, which was always given to him.

Although he had lost everything, the poor man had never lost his happy smile and cheerful manner, and passers-by gave him whatevever small coin they could spare. Until one day, when a rich merchant came past him and looked at him in disgust.

'You disgusting beggar,' he said and spat on the poor man. 'How dare you ask me to give you money? I am a high-born man, son of a lord and not born in filth as you were. Why should I give my hard-earned money to the likes of you who belongs in the gutter?'

He was about to walk on when the crippled man began to laugh. The rich merchant turned and aimed a kick at the beggar.

'Who do you think you are, beggar, to laugh at me, who is so high above you in the world?' The beggar took the kick without a sound and laughed again.

He said, 'I may be only half a man, Sir, but, as the Guru Nanak has said, all men are equal in the eyes of God. And did not the Guru Har Krishen, who was so young and yet so wise, say that all should help the needy? I am a man who is needy because I cannot help myself. You may not be a Sikh, one of the Khalsa like me, but you are still one of God's children.'

And the rich man was so ashamed that he filled the beggar's bowl with coins.

Songs

I'd like to teach the world to sing	*Apusskidu* 2
Love somebody	*Tinderbox* 16
Sing a song of people	*Tinderbox* 18

Thoughts to share

Think quietly about those people who, through no fault of their own, have little or no food to eat.

Let us be kind to everyone who needs kindness.

If we are able to help somebody, then we should.

Poem

'Take care – I am as good as you', page 205

83 At the time of Diwali *October/November*

Background

Diwali is one of several major festivals in the Hindu calendar and falls during the last week of October or the first week in November. The whole festival lasts five days and celebrates the return of the Prince Rama to the kingdom of Ayodhaya after fourteen years of exile.

He was sent into exile in the forest by his father, King Dasaratha, at the instigation of Rama's stepmother, Kaikeyi. When the exile was over, Rama and his wife, Sita, returned to take the throne. They were welcomed by the light of a thousand lamps, lit by the people of Ayadhaya.

Story

Rahim finds his Way Home

(This story has no origins in Hindu folklore, except to illustrate the joyous nature of the Festival)

'I am so cold and hungry,' cried Rahim to the cruel wind and savage snow that beat into his poor, sore face. He tried to get some warmth and comfort from the ragged robe that was wrapped round him.

The robe was made from wool woven from the fleecy sheep that munched the grass on the warm, green plains which he had left behind all those years before. But now, like him, the robe was old and thin and did little to keep out the biting cold of the mountains that stood between him and his home.

Rahim cried out to all the gods whose names he could remember to help him find his way back to his home village on the far side of these terrible mountains.

But no one answered. Rahim thought, in his misery, that perhaps he was being punished for leaving his home and family to seek his fortune in the bazaars of the Big City.

Rahim climbed ever higher, until he was struggling through deep snow that came up to his waist. It seemed to grow ever colder and the snow fell so heavily that it was like a white curtain. He could see nothing ahead. The poor traveller fell to his knees, so weary and cold that he thought he was going to die on these terrible slopes.

Then he saw the dancing light, a flickering flame that leapt and glowed in front of his unbelieving eyes. It seemed to hover only an arms-length in front of him, as if to invite him to follow its spritely dance.

And, because there was little else that he could do, Rahim let the flame lead him, he knew nor cared where. Then, as suddenly as it had appeared, the light was gone. The blizzard ceased, the wind fell.

Rahim cried out in joy and thanks as he saw, before him, hundreds and hundreds of lights in the valley, far below. Somehow, he stumbled down the mountain and into the village street. Everywhere he could see lamps burning, so that the village was one huge glow of welcome.

Great tears ran down Rahim's face. Not only was he home but he had arrived at a time of great celebration – the time that is called Diwali.

Songs

Diwali	*Tinderbox* 62
	Festivals Book 1
If you're happy	*Apusskidu* 1
Welcome home	*Tinderbox* 60

Thoughts to share

We are happy that we can share in the joy of other children, even though they may have different celebrations.

Diwali is a festival of light. Let us hope that all the world may share in the light that is brought by peace and love for one another.

Poem

'The Brightest Time of Year', page 205

84 At the time of Thanksgiving Day USA

November

Background

Americans celebrate the first harvest gathered by people from England after they had survived a long sea voyage, a terrible winter, a very hot summer and plague. It is, of course, a national holiday in the USA.

Narrative

The First Harvest in New England

In September 1620, a tiny ship called the *Mayflower* set sail from Plymouth in Devon, to sail 3000 miles (4800km) across the wild Atlantic Ocean. On board were 102 men, women and children, setting out to begin a new life in the unknown land called America.

The ship landed in America in November, after a very uncomfortable voyage. It was many months later, and many of the travellers had died from sickness, before the first harvest was gathered in.

Edward Winslow, one of the travellers, who are known as the Pilgrim Fathers, wrote to a friend in England. He described how houses had been built and how the settlers had sown peas, barley and Indian corn.

The crops had been hard to grow in the heat of an American summer, especially after a winter so cold that those who lived through it were grateful that they were able to tend the new plants. The peas and barley did not grow well but the struggling farmers were happy that the Indian corn had produced a good crop. This, at least, would help to feed the new Americans through the next winter.

The Pilgrim Fathers gave thanks to God for their first harvest in New England, as they called it. This part of America is still called New England and many of the towns have the same names as English towns. The American people still remember this first harvest because it was the beginning of their nation.

This celebration, held on the last Thursday in November, is a public holiday all over the USA. It is called Thanksgiving Day, and Americans try to celebrate it wherever they are, even in a foreign country.

The celebration is rather like our Christmas, and people give each other presents, hold family parties and eat turkey for dinner, often followed by pumpkin pie.

Songs

Harvest	*Harlequin* 31
I can see cherries	*Harlequin* 30
One potato, two potato	*Apusskidu* 31

Thoughts to share

Appreciate the world so sweet,
Be grateful for the food we eat;
Rejoice to hear the birds that sing,
Be glad for life, for everything.

Let us think how lucky we are to have plenty of food in our country.

May we do all we can to help hungry people in countries where there is war or famine.

Think quietly about all the food we enjoy because of the hard work of many people.

Poem
'Thanksgiving', page 206

85 At the time of Eid-el-Fitr

Lunar Islamic Year, 9th month

Background

Eid-el-Fitr means 'The Feast of the ending of the fast'. The fast is that which Muslims observe in the ninth month, Ramadan, of their calendar. During Ramadan, the only Muslims who are excused the fast are grown-ups who are ill, women who are expecting a baby and children under ten years of age. Others do not eat or drink between sunrise and sunset. The end of the fast is signalled by the appearance of the first new moon after Ramadan.

To celebrate, Muslims wear new clothes and send 'Blessed Festival' cards to one another, and they visit each others' homes. Children receive presents and money and it is a time of great celebration and enjoyment.

Story

The Poor Rich Man

(This story has no origins in Muslim doctrine or folklore nor does it relate to Islam in any way, except to relate to the 'pillar' of the Faith that requires Muslims to give money to charity.)

Once there was a very rich man whose name was Cyrus Skinflint. Not only was he rich but he was very mean. At night, he lit only one candle, carrying it from room to room with him.

He spent no money on clothes and went round his dark and dingy house, wearing an old suit that he had owned since he was a young man, many years before.

He went shopping once a month, always looking for bargains just as the market traders were packing up their stalls. He bought the fruit and vegetables that the traders were about to throw away, and he only bought the scraps of meat that the butchers sold as dog food.

He spent his days and evenings in counting his money – he kept it under a floorboard in his bedroom. Cyrus liked £50 notes because they did not take up a lot of room.

One day a woman, carrying a collecting box, knocked on the door of his gloomy old house. Cyrus Skinflint opened the door, just enough for the woman to see one eye and the tip of his long, red nose.

'What do you want?' he snapped.

'Would you like to give me some money for blind people, please?' asked the woman politely.

'No!' barked Skinflint, and slammed the door in her face.

The following week, a man, carrying a collecting box, knocked on the door of his gloomy old house.

Cyrus Skinflint opened the door, just enough for the man to see the lobe of one hairy ear and the end of his pointed chin.

'What do you want?' he snapped.

'Would you like to give me some money for starving people in Africa, please?' asked the man.

'No!' barked Skinflint, and slammed the door in his face.

During the next six months, Cyrus Skinflint refused to give money for old folk, the lifeboats, deaf people, disabled people and children who have no parents.

Then, one cold winter's night, Skinflint knocked his candle over and set fire to his curtains. In no time at all, the house burnt down. All his

£50 notes were burnt to ashes and he was left with nothing, only his pyjamas and dressing-gown.

But, to his surprise, people did everything they could to find him a home, and gave him money to buy clothes and furniture. Skinflint was very surprised because he had always thought that everyone was as mean as he was. And, as soon as he had got himself a job and some money he became a collector for 'Save the Children'. It had taken a dreadful happening for him to realise what a very mean person he had been.

Songs

When I needed a neighbour	*Someone's Singing, Lord*	35
With a little help from my friends	*Alleluya*	38
You and I	*Tinderbox*	55

Thoughts to share

We should remember that everyone needs someone.

Think quietly about people who have no friends or family.

Let us be grateful for all those people who give their time to collecting for charity.

Poem

'A Time of Happiness', page 206

86 At the time of Vesakha

First month in the Buddhist Lunar Year

Background

This is the most important festival in the Buddhist year and celebrates the life of the Buddha, the 'Enlightened One', Prince Siddhartha Gautama.

Buddhists live by Five Vows, including a promise not to harm any living thing.

Story

The Grumbly Animals

(This story has no origins in Buddhist doctrine or folklore nor does it relate to Buddhism in any way, except to the Vow that Buddhists will hurt no living thing.)

Long ago, when the world was very young, there were only thirteen animals. One day, they were called to a meeting by the god who had the job of looking after them. This god had no special name so we will call him 'The Keeper'.

The animals had been grumbling about their voices for two moons, and The Keeper was tired of hearing their grumbles. Bee did not like its hum, Cat its mew, Dog its bark, Elephant its trumpet, Fly its buzz, Goose its cackle, Horse its neigh, Lion its roar, Mouse its squeak, Owl its hoot, Pig its grunt, Sheep its bleat and Wolf its howl.

The Keeper listened to their grumbles and thought for a long time. Then he said, with a little godly smile, 'Mm. I think I can do something about that. How would it be if I took away your voices altogether. At least we would have a much more peaceful world. Besides, then I would not have to listen to your grumbling, would I?'

But the animals did not like this, not one little bit, and they made a dreadful noise telling The Keeper that it was a dreadful idea.

So The Keeper said, 'I'll tell you what I'll do. For seven days you shall all sing like sparrows. Then we shall see about your voices after that.' And, before the animals could think of anything to say, he had disappeared into thin air. Well, he was a god.

You never heard anything like the world for the next week. Can you imagine Lion opening his great mouth which is full of big teeth and chirping *Tweet Tweet*? Or Horse trotting across the field, chirping *Tweet Tweet* as she ran? Or Elephant lifting her trunk and chirping *Tweet Tweet*?

The animals were all very glad when seven days had passed and they all found they had new voices.

Bee howled, Cat bleated, Dog grunted, Elephant hooted, Fly neighed, Goose barked, Horse mewed, Lion squeaked, Mouse roared, Owl buzzed, Pig cackled, Sheep trumpeted and Wolf hummed. All the animls had a wonderful time trying out their new voices.

This was fine for a while. Then they all started to poke fun at one another. In no time at all, tempers began to show and, soon, all the animals were fighting instead of poking fun.

Before they could do too much damage to one another, The Keeper had to come along and give them back their proper voices.

You will be pleased to know that, when the animals had been given back their proper voices, they saw just how stupid they had been and that they should have been satisfied with their own voices in the first place.

All the animals have kept their own voices, ever since. And, if you think about it, have *you* ever heard a fly neighing or a mouse roaring?

Songs

All things which live below the sky	*Someone's Singing, Lord* 41
The animals went in two by two	*Apuuskidu* 38
The ants go marching one by one	*Okki-tokki-unga* 36

Thoughts to share

Let us not be afraid of little creatures but take care they neither bite nor sting us because they do not think as we do.

Do you think that our pets love us only because we feed them?

Poem

'Hurt no Living Thing', page 207

Appendix 1: Poems for special occasions

Assembly 69: New Year

First Foot

One... two... three... four...
Midnight knocking at our door.

A tall, dark stranger waits outside
Turning away, his face to hide.

A lump of coal in one black hand –
What does it mean? Why does he stand

Holding out his hand to us all
As we welcome him into the midnight hall?

Goodbye to the old year, good luck in the new,
'Come in, dear friend, peace be with you.'

Ian Serraillier

Assembly 70: Shrove Tuesday

Pancake Day!

Beat the batter
in the bowl.
Heat the butter
in the pan.
Toss the pancake
if you can.

In the Shrovetide
pancake races
pancake experts
show their paces.
Pancakes dropped
or held aloft,
Pancakes proud
Pancakes flopped.

With watering mouths
and hunger hearty
we will have
a pancake party.
Cram as many
as you can –
some with treacle
some with jam.

Pancakes fat.
Pancakes neat.
Piles of pancakes.
Eat, eat, eat.

Ann Bonner

Assembly 71: Mother's Day – Two Cinquains

Mothers

Mothers
Can be a pain
But have you stopped to think
That you might be a bigger pain
To Her?

Children
Should love Mother,
Because you will never
Have another Mother like her
Again.

Assembly 72: Easter

Easter

This is the end of Winter's reign
When the squirrel had to hide,
When the swallows fled to the south
And all the Summer flowers died:
When the snow took over the mountain tops,
When the frost had the fields in an iron hold,
When ice shut the swans out of the ponds
And the world was imprisoned by cold.
Winter has passed: the birds return,
The seed beneath the stone has found
A way to the light and like a knife
The daffodil prises open the ground.
Buds and bulbs break out of their bonds
And squirrels were only sleeping and survive
By the yearly miracle
That keeps the world alive.

Stanley Cook

Assembly 73: The eve of St George's Day

A Dragon's Lament

It isn't much fun to find out you're a dragon,
I wish I'd been born St George.
I would laze about town drinking wine from a flagon,
Then look for poor creatures to scourge.
I'd have a head start with my sword and my armour,
No dragon would *dare* to advance;
And dozens of maidens I'd save before supper,
If only they'd give me the chance.
I'm the last of my kind;
You'd think they'd want to preserve me,
For I'm tired and flameless and old.
I'd give a few puffs
And then roll over gently
And hope that the blade isn't cold.

St. George, he'll be famous,
But what of the dragon?
Who will remember my name?
Ah, such is this world –
They must all have their heroes,
And dragons are always fair game.

Trevor Harvey

Assembly 74: May Day

The Maypole

Twirl your ribbons
   as you go
in and out
   the Maypole...
Let the colours
   twist and flow
in and out
   the Maypole!
Skip and rally,
   turn about,
round and round
   the Maypole...
Outside in
   and inside out –
round and round
   the Maypole...

Now, the season's
   crowned and blessed –
all her rites
   attended –
Stands the Maypole
   fully dressed,
and the dance
   is ended!

   And the dance
      is
         ended...

Jean Kenward

Assembly 75: Harvest

Cruel Winter

Cruel Winter is coming,
Dormouse fattens himself
For the long sleep.
Farmer gathers harvest
And looks to his sheep.
Squirrel gathers food
For winter store,
Swallows mass and wing
Their way to warmer shore –
Cruel Winter is coming.

(See also Assembly 84, 'Thanksgiving USA')

Assembly 76: Hallowe'en

Trick or Treat?

A night for trick or treat,
A night to joke or beg for sweets.
Pumpkin head shines candle bright,
Flickering eyes that ask the night
What celebration goes on here?
Why do children practise fear?
Do you frighten old and young
Just because you think it's fun?
Beware, lest you should choose to call
On folk who are afraid of all
Those things so funny to a kid.
You might be done by
As you did!

Assembly 77: Guy Fawkes Night: Five Haiku

Fireworks

See how the flames rise
Smoke makes the night cough huskily,
Sprite-like sparklers dance.

Catherine wheel spins,
Stabbed by cruel nail
Revolves, giddy, dead.

Guy blackens and sags,
His bonds well charred, slack, dropping,
What is he worth now?

Star-high stream rockets,
Tails ablaze, heads bursting bright,
Silver stars fall, die, gone.

The bonfire wearies
Of pleasing watching children,
And goes dark, sulking.

Assembly 78: Christmas Carols

Sing a Carol

See the angel on the tree,
See the lights that glow so bright,
For the baby born to Mary
On that far-off Christmas night.
See the baby in the manger,
See the shepherds leave their sheep,
Baby Jesus born to save us,
Holy Infant lies asleep.
Sing a carol for His birthday,
Sing his praises loud and clear,
Glory to the Child's arrival,
Worship for the baby dear.

Assembly 79: Christmas Trees

Trees for Sale

Buy-me tree,
Take-home tree
Fairy-topped tree,
Silver-glitter tree
Cheer-bright tree,
Warm-tree indoors
Laughing at the snow.
Sparkle-tree, shimmer-tree, happy-tree,
Potted tree
Trapped tree,
Dusty tree fallen over.
No-needle tree,
Naked tree,
No tree.

Assembly 80: Chinese New Year: Five Haiku

Lion Dance

Ho! Paper Lion
Frantic dancing for New Year
Be it Rat or Snake.

A frightening head
Lashing, twisting its long tail,
Smoke puffing from nose.

Paper beast jump leap
The dragon's legs are human!
See the bulging eyes.

Is the dragon real?
Red and gold and green and blue
Gong and drum make noise.

Hear the New Year din,
Dragons dance the New Year in,
And all shall enjoy!

Assembly 81: Hanukah Tanka

Rejoice for Light

Rejoice! I see light
And hear a celebration joy,
A bright, dancing flame.
It tells us that Hanukah's here
And we merrily sing and dance.

Assembly 82: Baisakhi: Sonnet

Take Care – I am as Good as You

Long spotted Snake slips through the tall, wet grass,
As Giraffe stamps her foot with angry thud
And says, 'Why do you wriggle as I pass
Squirming as you slide by me in the mud?'
Spotted Snake says, 'Who do you think you are
So far above me, almost out of sight?
Do not forget, from your great height so far,
If I so choose, your ankle I can bite.
I too can see the sun as it climbs high
Do not be rude to others who pass by.'

Assembly 83: Diwali Haiku

The Brightest Time of Year

Hurry, light the lamps!
Bright Diwali has come to say
'Brighten up the sky!'

Assembly 84: Thanksgiving Day USA

Thanksgiving

Thank you
  for all my hands can hold –
    apples red,
     and melons gold,
      yellow corn
        both ripe and sweet
        peas and beans
         so good to eat!

Thank you
  for all my eyes can see –
    lovely sunlight,
     field and tree,
      white cloud boats
      in sea-deep sky,
        soaring bird and butterfly.

Thank you
  for all my ears can hear –
    birds' songs echoing
    far and near,
     songs of little
      stream, big sea,
       cricket, bullfrog,
       duck and bee!

Ivy O. Eastwick

Assembly 85: Eid-el-Fitr Cinquain

A Time of Happiness

Be glad!
For now Ramadan,
The long fast, is over.
Eid has come and we are happy.
Be glad!

Assembly 86: Vesakha

Hurt no Living Thing

Hurt no living thing;
Ladybird, nor butterfly,
Nor moth with dusty wing,
Nor cricket chirping cheerily,
Nor grasshopper so light of leap,
Nor dancing gnat, nor beetle fat,
Nor harmless worms that creep.

Christina Rossetti

Appendix 2: Mood Music

'Mood' music is usually 'coming in' and 'going out' music, or, more formally, 'processional' and ' recessional'. You may want music to create an atmosphere, although one cannot say with any degree of conviction that all infant children are susceptible to atmospheric music.

For many assemblies, you do not need much more than a background music. These suggestions are drawn from the lighter classical work and the world of popular music, most of it elderly – contemporary pop has little to offer in the way of a message.

Teachers who use mood music have to rely on the in-school resources, their own collections and library or advisory sources. Hence, these suggestions are by way of a hit or miss offering and it is a matter of chance as to whether you can find them. Most of the tracks are to be found on various compilations but, because of the wide scope of the suggestions, teachers can only expect to track down some of the ideas.

Music Advisory Services may be able to help in providing music resource, if you do consider music to be a significant part of your assemblies.

The most one can expect is the creation of an atmosphere which approaches your aim and hope that the children absorb the nature of the emotion that you are trying to engender. If in doubt, it is best to use 'calm' music, from whatever source.

Classical Music

* Use an instrumental version in multi-faith assemblies

General	Excerpts from
Albinoni, Giazotto	Adagio
Bach J S	Air on a G-string
	* Jesu, Joy Of Man's Desiring
	* Sheep may Safely Graze (arr Kramer)
Beethoven	Moonlight Sonata
Bizet	Carmen Suite No 2 'Habanera'
Borodin	Polovtzian Dances
Britten	Sea Pictures (from Peter Grimes)
Chopin	Fantasie-Impromptu in C sharp minor Op 66

Copland	Outdoor Overture
Debussy	Children's Corner Suite
	Clair de Lune
	Prelude a l'apres midi d'un faune
Faure	Dolly Suite
	* 'Sanctus' from Requiem
Fibich	Poeme
Javanese Gamelan	Music from the Morning of the World
Godard	* Berceuse (Angels Guard Thee) from Jocelyn
Gounod	* O Divine Redeemer
Grieg	Peer Gynt Suite No 1 Op 46 (Morning Mood)
Handel	Largo
Humperdinck	* 'Evening Prayer' from Hansel and Gretel
Massenet	'Meditation' from Thais
McDowell	To a Wild Rose
Mozart, W.A.	Eine kleine Nachtmusik
	Violin Concerto No.5 in A major
Mozart, Leopold	Toy Symphony
Offenbach	Baccarolle
Orff	Opening of Carmina Burana
Pachelbel	Canon in D
Ravel	Bolero
	Pavane pour une infante defunte
Schumann	Carnaval
	1st movement Symphony No 1 (Spring)
	Traumeri
Strauss, Johann II	Waltzes (Any)
Stravinsky	Circus Polka
Tchaikowsky	Italian Caprice
	Nutcracker Suite
	Romeo and Juliet
	Swan Lake
Vaughan Williams	The Lark Ascending
John Williams	Theme from Star Wars

Popular Music

(Most of these songs will have been performed by other artists too.)

Adler, Larry	Genevieve
Armstrong, Louis	What a Wonderful World
Beatles	All You Need is Love
	Here Comes The Sun
Ball, Kenny	March of the Siamese Children
	(from *The King and I* – Jazz version)
Baskett	Zip-a-dee-doo-dah
Bilk, Acker	Stranger on the Shore (Clarinet)
Brubeck, Dave	Take Five
Conway, Russ	Roulette (Piano)
Crosby, Bing	Swingin' On A Star
Faith, Percy	Theme from a 'A Summer Place'
Foster & Allen	The Birdie Song (Accordion)
Karas, Anton	Cafe Mozart Waltz (Zither)
	Harry Lime Theme (Zither)
Mantovani	Swedish Rhapsody
Morgan, Russ	Cruising down the River
New Vaudeville Band	Winchester Cathedral
Shand, Jimmy	Bluebell Polka
Smith, Whistling Jack	I was Kaiser Bill's Batman
Tollefsen, Tora	Hora Staccato (Accordion)
Traditional	Amazing Grace
Zabach, Florian	Hot Canary (Violin)

Ideas for music for specific assemblies

	Theme	Artist/Composer	Music
1	New term	Abba	Arrival
2	Our school	The Spinners	Morning has Broken
3	School creed	John Williams	New Sun Rising
4	Home address	Havergal Brian	Trotting to Market
5	Left & right	Johann Strauss I	Radetzky March
6	Early to bed	Russ Morgan	So Tired
7	Too much TV	Schostakovitch	Symphony No 15 (end)
8	Matches	Scriabin	Prometheus, Poem of Fire

9 Tablets	Havergal Brian	Gargoyles
10 Absenteism	Haydn	Clock Symphony, 2nd movement
11 Asking	Julie Andrews	Supercalifragilistic-expialidocious
12 Bullying	Lei Zhen-bang	Chinese Martial Arts
13 Excuses	Elsie Carlisle	Little Man, You've had a Busy Day
14 Listening	Orff	Carmina Burana (Opening)
15 Listening	Chopin	Fantasie Impromptu
16 Punctuality	Radio Revellers	My Grandfather's Clock
17 Rules	Scott Joplin	Stoptime Rag
18 Teasing	Henry Mancini	It's Easy to Say (from Film 10)
19 Building sites	Trini Lopez	If I had a Hammer
20 In the country	Cyril Ornandel	Tale of Peter Rabbit
21 Flowers	Grainger	English Country Garden
22 Graffiti	Johann Strauss	Waltz, Artist's Life
23 Litter	Pee Wee Hunt	Twelfth Street Rag
24 Swimming	Schumann	Symphony No 1 1st Movement (Spring)
25 Tidiness	Mozart	Rondo from Horn Concerto No 4
26 Vandalism	Widor	Toccata, Organ Symphony No 5
27 Anticipation	Rimsky-Korsakov	March of the Golden Cockerel
28 Kingsley	Dowland	Lachrimae Antiquae
29 Shaftesbury	Gounod	Soldiers' Chorus from 'Faust'
30 Races	The Spinners	The Family of Man
31 Humanity	Roberto Inglez	The Green Cockatoo
32 Pets	Saint Saens	Carnival of the Animals
33 Advice	Eric Coates	Three Bears Suite
34 Apologising	Kalmar, Ruby, Snyder	Who's Sorry Now?
35 Boasting	Mantovani	Beautiful Dreamer

36 Caring	Johnny Mercer	Friendship
37 Cooperation	Edwards, Nichols & Bentley	Little Red Monkey
38 Envy	Peter Bilk	If
39 Individual worth	Bing Crosby	Swingin' on a Star
40 Gossip	Whispering	Roy Fox
41 Gratitude	Aled Jones	If I can Help Somebody
42 Nosiness	Vienna Musical Ensemble	A Musical Joke
43 Politeness	Petula Clarke	Christopher Robin
44 Persuasion	Javanese Gavelan	Ramayan Monkey Chant
45 Promises	Geoff Love	When I See an Elephant Fly (from *Dumbo*, Walt Disney)
46 Self-importance	Washington Harline	When you Wish upon a Star
47 Selfishness	Gerry Marsden	You'll never Walk Alone
48 Sharing	Malcolm Arnold	Tam O'Shanter
49 Stealing by finding	The Shadows	Genie with the Light Brown Lamp
50 Winners & losers	Schubert	Marche Militaire
51 Action not words	Gershwin	Nice Work if You Can Get It
52 Confession	John Inman	The Teddy Bears' Picnic
53 Boredom	Richard Strauss	Also Sprach Zarathustra
54 Remembering	Andrew Lloyd Webber	Memory (from *Cats*)
55 Contentment	Luton Girls' Choir	Count your Blessings
56 Determination	Jerome Kern	Pick yourself up
57 Fear	Nicola LeFane	Invisible Places
58 Good intentions	Mario Ruiz Armengol	Perhaps, Perhaps, Perhaps
59 Over-indulgence	Jing Ying Soloists	Birdsong
60 Honesty	Richard Clayderman	People
61 Lies	Ink Spots	It's a Sin to Tell a Lie
62 Luck	Band of the RAF	Reach for the Sky

63 Keep trying	Roger Webb	Best that You Can (Arthur's Theme)
64 Patience	Walt Disney	Give a Little Whistle (from *Pinocchio*)
65 Applejacks	Tell me When	Judgement
66 Completing jobs	Walt Disney	Heigh Ho (from *Snow White*)
67 Procrastination	Vera Lynn	It's a Lovely Day Tomorrow
68 Self-denigration	Rimsky Korsakov	Flight of the Bumble Bee
69 New Year	Cyril Ornandel	Tale of Peter Rabbit
70 Pancake Day	David Rose	Holiday for Strings
71 Mother's Day	Billy Cotton	Ma, I Miss your Apple Pie
72 Easter	Irving Berlin	Easter Parade
73 St George's Day	Clannad	Robin (the Hooded Man)
74 May Day	Beadell, Tollerton	Cruising down the River
75 Harvest	Aaron Copland	Outdoor Overture
76 Hallowe'en	Havergal Brian	The Hag
77 Bonfire Night	Handel	Music for the Royal Fireworks
78/79 Christmas	Any appropriate carols	
80 Chinese New Year	Lyrichord label	Chinese Drums and Gongs
81 Hanukah	Argon label	Songs and Dances from Israel
82 Baisakhi	Argon label	Religions of India
83 Diwali	EMI	Raga Rang
84 Thanksgiving USA	Charles Ives	Putnam's Camp (from Three Places in New England)
85 Lyrichord label	Eid-el-Fitr	Folk Music of Iran
86 Vesakha	Lyrichord label	Offering to the Guru Drakman

Appendix 3: Songs

Source Books

1 A & C Black Song Books

Alleluya   Apusskidu   Harlequin   Tthe Jolly Herring
Okki-tokki-unga   Someone's Singing, Lord   Tinderbox

2 New Child Songs (National Curriculum Education council)

Songs for General Use

(Action songs marked *)

A better world	*Alleluya*	60
At half past three we go home to tea	*Someone's Singing, Lord*	58
Birthday song	*Tinderbox*	59
Both sides now	*Alleluya*	33
Can anyone tell me that	*Alleluya*	32
Click goes the switch	*New Child Songs*	33
Father, we thank you for the night	*New Child Songs*	32
Give to us eyes	*Someone's Singing, Lord*	18
God made the world	*New Child Songs*	3
* Growing	*BBC Play School Songbook*	5
Here we come with gladness	*New Child Songs*	82
* How do you feel today?	*BBC Play School Songbook*	1
I danced in the morning	*Someone's Singing, Lord*	29
* If you're happy	*Apusskidu*	1
I'm very glad of God	*Someone's Singing, Lord*	22
Join in the game	*Okki Tokki Unga*	2
* Let's all be happy – Maja pade	*Tinderbox*	57
Let's beat a song of praise	*New Child Songs*	71
* Let's pretend	*Tinderbox*	25
* Make a face	*Tinderbox*	3
Look up	*New Child Songs*	1
Morning has broken	*Someone's Singing, Lord*	3
Music Man, The	*Okki-tokki-unga*	44
* Mysteries	*Tinderbox*	40
New things to do	*Tinderbox*	58
O Lord! Shout for Joy	*Someone's Singing, Lord*	4
One man's hands	*Alleluya*	61

I am a Person

What a Life!

House and Home

Friends and Neighbours

The World around us

Round the Year

Or any song from Harlequin

Animals and Things

Festivals

Shrove Tuesday (Pancake Day)

Mothers' Day

Easter

St George's Day

May Day

Traditional Harvest (see also *Thanksgiving*)

Ears of corn are waving	*New Child Songs*	22
Look for signs that summer's done	*Someone's Singing, Lord*	54
* Song of the Seed	*BBC Play School Songbook*	2
The farmer comes to scatter the seed	*Someone's Singing, Lord*	56
We plough the fields and scatter	*New Child Songs*	93
When the corn is planted	*Someone's Singing, Lord*	55

Christmas

Any songs from:	*Carol, Gaily Carol* (A & C Black)	
	Merrily to Bethlehem (A & C Black)	

At the time of the Chinese New Year

Can't help but wonder	*Alleluya*	34
Chinatown dragon	*Harlequin*	24
New things to do	*Tinderbox*	58

At the time of Hanukah

Hanukah	*Harlequin*	39
Sing a sing of people	*Tinderbox*	18

At the time of Diwali

Diwali	*Tinderbox*	62

At the time of Thanksgiving USA (See also *Traditional Harvest*)

Harvest	*Harlequin*	31
I can see cherries	*Harlequin*	30

At the time of Eid-el-Fitr

With a little help from my friends	*Alleluya*	38
You and I	*Tinderbox*	55

At the time of Vesakha

All things which live below the sky	*Someone's Singing, Lord*	41

Appendix 4:
Are you listening, God?

Prayers for all occasions

Dear God, we shall have this day only once. Help us not to waste it.

Dear Father, may we be kind and loving in all we do.

Father of us all, bless and keep us safe from harm.

Father God, please be our friend.

Father God, please make us brave children.

Please God, forgive us for the times when we have been unkind to others.

Thank you, Father, for all the wonderful things on our earth.

Dear God, help us to do all the good we can in all the ways that we can.

Father God, may we learn to help one another.

Thank you, Father, for health and strength.

Father God, teach us which is right and which is wrong.

Just Me, God

Father God, be good to me. I am so small and the world is so big.

Dear God, give me helping hands and a loving heart.

Please, God, forgive me for not doing those things that I should have done.

Please, God, forgive me for doing those things that I should not have done.

Lord of the loving heart, make my heart loving, too.

Please be near me, Father, when I need You.

May we do the things we should,
To be to others kind and good;
In all we do in work or play
To grow more loving every day.

The People around Us

Dear God, please help all those people who are unhappy today, wherever they may be.

Lord, please help those people who have no food to eat and no pure water to drink.
Father God, please help those people who have no homes.
Father God, please help those people who are ill.
Father God, please help those people who are alone.
Father God, please help those people who are afraid.
Father God, please help those people who are sad.

Dear Father of our world family, please love and care for children everywhere.

Lord God, Father of us all, show us how to love one another.

This is our School

Thank you, Father for our school.

Father, please bless our school.

Thank you, Father, for all the people who care for us in school.

Thank you, Father, for our teachers and all those who help us to learn about Your world.

We thank you, Father, for all the new things we learn in our school.

Father God, help me to try hard with my lessons.

Lord, this is our school. Help us to make it a safe and caring place.
Father, show us how to make our school a loving and caring place.

The World about Us

Thank you, Father, for all flowers and trees and everything that grows.

Dear God, show us what is beautiful and good in this world.

Father God, teach us to look after the places where we learn and play and live.

Dear God, thank you for parks and playgrounds and all the places where we play.

Father, teach us how to look after the places where we play.

Father God, help us to make the world a cleaner place.

Teach us, Lord, to care about the cities, towns and villages in which we live.

People

Thank you, Father, for all those people who keep us safe from harm.

Thank you, God, for all those men and women who care for us when danger is about.

Thank you, God, for those men and women who look after us when we are ill.

Thank you, God, for all those men and women who grow and transport and prepare our food.

Thank you, God, for all those men and women who keep our towns and cities and villages clean and tidy.

Thank you, Father, for everyone who looks after other people.

Things that Grow

Thank you, Father, for flowers and trees.

Teach us, Father, to care about trees and flowers and never to damage them because we think it is fun.

Thank you, God, for the birds and all wild animals.

Thank you, Father, for our pets. Help us to care for them properly.

A School Creed

This is our school,
Let peace live here.
Let the rooms be full of happiness.
Let love be all around,
Love of one another,
Love of all people,
And love of life and living.
Let us remember
That as many hands build a house,
So many hearts make a school.

A Child's Prayer (based on the Lord's Prayer)

Father God, who is everywhere,
Your name is very special.
You are with us now
And always will be.
Please care for us because we are small
And you are great.
We are sorry for doing wrong things
And we will try to forgive others
Just as you forgive us.
Make us good children
And keep us safe from harm.

The Lord's Prayer (*Matthew 6, New English Bible version, 1970*)

Our Father in heaven,
thy name be hallowed;
thy kingdom come,
thy will be done,
on earth as in heaven.
Give us today our daily bread.
Forgive us the wrong we have done,
as we have forgiven those who have wronged us.
And do not bring us to the test,
But save us from the evil one.
Amen

Prayers for the Close of School

O let us see another day;
Bless us all this night we pray
And to the sun we all will bow
And say 'Goodbye', but just for now.

Eli Jenkins' prayer from Under Milk Wood *by Dylan Thomas*

As we go Home

Lord, keep us safe this night,
Secure from all our fears,
Your strength to guard us while we sleep
'Til morning light appears.

Now the day is over,
Night is drawing near,
Lord, keep us as we sleep tonight,
With You we know no fear.

Blessings for the close of assembly

May God keep us safe and happy today and every day.

Bless us, Lord and look after us all today and every day.

May the blessing of Almighty God go with us all today.

Blessings for the close of School

Father, keep us safe this night.

May God bless us and keep us through this night.

May Almighty God bless us and guard us and keep us all through the night.

Please bless us, Lord, as we go home.

May God bless us and keep us through the night to come and in all the days that follow.

Appendix 5: Useful assembly books for infant and first school assemblies

Active Assemblies for the National Curriculum	Tracey & Dinsdale	Schofield and Sims
Assemblies A–Z	Ward	Stanley Thornes
Assemblies for Primary Schools (Autumn, Spring & Summer Terms – 3 books)	Cooling	RMEP
Assemblies for Primary Schools	Brandling	Stanley Thornes
It's Our Assembly		
It's Our Turn for Assembly	Farncombe	NCEC
Let's Plan an Assembly		
The Autumn Assembly Book		
The Spring Assembly Book	Brandling	Stanley Thornes
The Summer Assembly Book		
Assembly Kit	Wood	Longman
The Assembly Year	Fisher	Collins
First Assemblies	Purton & Storey	Simon & Schuster (OP)
Good Morning, Everybody	Brandling	Stanley Thornes
Infant Assembly Book	Vause	Stanley Thornes
Join with Us 1 & 2	Jackson	Stanley Thornes
Share our World	Jackson	Stanley Thornes
Through the Year	Wilcock	Stanley Thornes
Tinderbox Assembly Book	Barrett	A & C Black
Together Today	Fisher	Evans
A World of Light	Price & Parmiter	Schofield & Sims

Further suggestions for Song Books

Children Praising	OUP
Come and Praise	BBC
Come and Sing	Scripture Union
Every Colour Under the Sun	Ward Lock
Flying a Round (rounds & partner songs)	A & C Black
Hymns and Songs for Children	National Society
Mango Spice (Caribbean songs)	A & C Black
Merrily to Bethlehem (Carols)	A & C Black
Morning has Broken	Schofield & Sims
Musical Calendar of Festivals	Ward Lock
New Child Songs	NCEC
Oxford Book of Carols	OUP
Sing a Song of Celebration	Holt, Rinehard & Winston 1984
Sing a Song 1 and 2	Nelson
Songs of Praise	OUP
Ta-ra-ra boom-de-ay	A & C Black